INspired Leadership

Presents

An INspired Evolution

9 WAYS TO GROW INTO YOUR GREATEST SELF

Rachel Thalmann

An INspired Evolution

© ESSDACK 2016 All Rights Reserved

ESSDACK 1500 E. 11th • Hutchinson, KS 67501
(620)663-9566

No part of this book may be reproduced or transmitted in any form whatsoever, electronic or mechanical, including photocopying, recording, or by any information storage and/or retrieval system, without written permission from the author, except for reviews.

www.inspiredleadershipwithin.com

The greatness that INspired Leadership recognizes can't be achieved. You can't earn it. It cannot be bought. It cannot be found "out there" somewhere. This greatness need only be discovered, uncovered, and unveiled – because it has always been inside you. Explore nine insights to help magnify your greatness and evolve into the greatest version of yourself.

ISBN: 978-0-692-69319-3

Cover design by Lori Blaine

Cover photo by Phoebe Janzen

Printed by Baker Bros.

For my dad, Steve Janzen

Acknowledgments

I never understood the magnitude of an acknowledgment page until I wrote this book. Writing a book requires occupied head and heart space for a long period of time, and many people are either involved in those spaces or left to manage the rest of the neglected spaces so a message can come to fruition. It is with gratitude that I sit here and think of people who have played a part to shape and form this message.

I'm thankful for an INspiring team: Tamara Konrade, Tammy Fellers, Mike Sanders, and Meg Wilson. I love you professionally and personally! Being part of a team that functions with high energy, enthusiasm, passion, great care, and recognizes a Higher Coach is deeply rewarding.

Thank you to ESSDACK, a supportive organization that knows how to work hard and play hard and provides an open and free range for people to create and grow and love what they do!

I'm deeply grateful to Jon McGraw and Russ Rausch for wholeheartedly receiving me into your work.

Thank you, Jessica Hoskinson for being so amazingly vulnerable. I never doubt the INL process because of you! Thanks, Greg Doudna, for writing your own rules and for letting me tell about it. I'm so glad I met you. Thank you, Brandon Clark, for eagerly sharing your success on a whim. Win the day!

Thank you, Mom, for encouraging creativity and demonstrating how to forge ahead. Thank you, Dad, for 36 years of support and for teaching in death why living is important.

Thank you to my loving and loyal husband, Drew, for cooking dinner so many evenings! I'm grateful for my kids, Abby and Jake, who unknowingly help me evolve day to day.

Thanks, Trish Pickard, for being a steady support. (Everyone needs a mentor!) Thank you, Eldon Wagler and Carol Duerksen, for accepting a random request to read this book and contributing insight. Thank you, Deb Haneke, for time, reflection, and amazing feedback! Thank you, Lori Blaine, for sitting patiently with us through the design process.

I want to mention, with love, the names of friends and family who have influenced me in one way or another: Amy, Amanda, Steven, Leslie, Robin, Renae, Rochelle, Polly, T.J., Stefan, Alicia, Jamie, Patti, Levi, and Trish.

I thank God, who is good and loving, for showing Himself to me as such.

It is also with deep gratitude that I think of you, reader, for choosing this book.

Contents

Prologue — *xi*

Introduction — *1*

Using this Book — *3*

Chapter One: **Your Story** — 5

Chapter Two: **Detached Involvement** — 17

Chapter Three: **Judgment** — 30

Chapter Four: **Rewrite Your Rules** — 43

Chapter Five: **Shhh…Listen!** — 60

Chapter Six: **The Gift of Intuition** — 70

Chapter Seven: **Mindful versus Mind Full** — 81

Chapter Eight: **Who is on Your Team?** — 97

Chapter Nine: **Something More** — 112

Epilogue — *127*

More about INspired Leadership — *130*

Prologue

The creation of a thousand forests is in one acorn.
— Ralph Waldo Emerson

Introduction

Just like an acorn is predestined to be a powerful oak tree, you are predestined with greatness inside you. The only prerequisite to becoming the greatness is to be aware in the moment to recognize it. For most of us this is a process, an evolution.

Within whatever shell you exist, there is part of you that is greater than that shell. Most people identify with the shell – the body and the mind – and if you find yourself focusing mostly on the external, that's okay. This book will probably inspire you most. Just know that beyond external form is a connection with a constant unseen River of Living Water…a constant Source of growth…and when rooted into that Source, real growth begins.

In the case of INspired Leadership, "real growth" means from the inside out, from the unseen to the seen. This often feels counterintuitive to most who are driven to make visible external changes in search of the internal feeling they actually desire.

During the discovery of the greatness within you, a bit of the process may be uncomfortable. For one, the safety of the shell will be compromised. To grow more deeply, the shell has to crack to allow for roots to develop. While this stage in evolution may cause fear or discomfort or vulnerability, it is the beginning of something vast and magnificent and strong.

What is most important to know about this journey is this: This greatness can't be achieved. You can't earn it. It cannot be bought. It cannot be found "out there" somewhere. This greatness need only be discovered, uncovered, and unveiled – because it has always been inside you.

May these INspired insights help "Magnify Your Greatness."

Using this Book

Each chapter is separated into *Acorn* and *Oak*.

The *Acorn* is the conceptual idea – the thing that's planted.

The *Oak* is what manifests when the acorn (the idea) has grown roots and evolved – it produces fruit that multiplies.

Wherever you find yourself in this process, my desire for you is this: *Love each moment. This moment* is where an INspired evolution begins.

Chapter 1

Your Story

The stories we tell literally make the world. If you want to change the world, you need to change your story. The truth applies both to individuals and to institutions.

– Michael Margolis

Your mind is constantly telling a story with or without your permission. It narrates what it sees and begins to label and file its interpretations. The efficiency of the amazing machine we call the brain is what gives human beings creative and critical thinking. We can use this to our advantage when we are mindful and engaged, but most of the time our brains function without our conscious knowledge.

As children, we learned the way the world works through our experiences and encounters with parents and family. To "survive" in this world, our brains worked on our behalf by creating stories and making sense of situations to keep us safe while providing the way out of situations that seemed like potential harm. Over time we learned to view the external world as we are, not as it is. I wear a pair of glasses for "Rachel" and you wear a pair just for you. All of our experiences and thoughts, and even unconscious thoughts, give us a certain view – our own. Wayne Dyer describes this phenomenon: "Loving people live in a loving world. Hostile people live in a hostile world. Same world."[1]

How can people living in the same community watch the same event and come up with totally different perspectives?

Here's why: When there is missing data, our brains automatically fill in the gaps.

It's a protective mechanism built into us – a way to stay alert to potential harm. It uses previously filed information to tell a story that makes the most sense according to previous experiences.

The part where this automatic system gets in the way of happiness is when it induces stress by the stories it tells – because most of them are negative – especially if your experiences led your brain to believe that safety and connection and belonging have been lacking in the past. If that is the case, it will lead you to see the same lack in the present.

You know the co-worker who didn't smile at you in the hall, and you made up a story he or she was mad at you? You know the meeting you attended when your idea was tabled for another day, and you made up the story your work wasn't valued? You know when your kid was left out of a Facebook post, and you made up the story that it was intentional and your kid's worthiness was being challenged? What about the time your spouse got a text that could've been interpreted harmlessly, but you told yourself the story that it was something more? Yeah…all made up.

The stories *feel* true, which is why we have an emotional response, but they're just a story…your interpretation of an event. And more than likely you acted on that story in a way that created evidence to make your story true, which induced unnecessary stress.

How true is your story?

What evidence do you have for the details in your story? If feedback or a different perspective is needed to determine the truth of the story, then have a conversation.

A friend told me that after her divorce she believed she'd greatly disappointed her grandpa, whom she dearly loves. He essentially held the role of a father in her life, so this story became significant because disappointing him felt painful. She began to internalize the idea that her grandpa's love for her had drastically decreased – even to the point of verbalizing to others, "Grandpa hates me!" Without consciously realizing, she increased the energy to the story. It *felt* true. After years of living with the story and indwelling belief of hatred, she had a conversation. "It was probably one of the most courageous moments…asking a man of often brash and vocal opinions, which he seemed to wear on his sleeve," she said. Until she overcame fear and courageously asked, it had been unclear to that point that the story was just that – a story.

Her grandfather's response set her free from the damaging effects of the story her brain had created.

In that moment not only was she released from years of self-judgment, but she discovered courage in asking for evidence if she became aware of stories again.

If you believe your story strongly enough, evidence to back it up will reveal itself and you will continue to feed the story with your own energy. Coincidently, when you're ready to become aware of the story and change it, evidence in favor of that decision will also reveal itself.

To become fully aware of the story, step back and listen. What is your internal dialogue? What are common themes in which you communicate? There is a space you can create, called awareness, that allows for objective observation. Many get lost in their thoughts and listen to the storyteller in their head without questioning it. If you can have a thought while having an awareness of that thought, then *you* are not your thoughts. Need to re-read that sentence? *You* are not your thoughts. *You* are the awareness behind your thoughts. *You* are the *essence* in that shell, not the shell itself. To become aware of this phenomenon is to become aware of your inherent greatness.

Why we tell stories

For many, storytelling began with something that happened in the past. We identify with an event or belief and retell the story over and over, giving the story more energy and hold over us in the present. *I've always been this way* is an obvious indication the past has defined your present. Clinging to the past will never allow you space to rewrite your story in the present. Your fullest potential was within you before the story began to unfold. Folding the past back up and putting it in your back pocket will allow you to reconnect with who you are right now – who you were before the storytelling in your mind began.

To bring your story to the surface, say out loud to yourself (or studies show greater sustained change occurs by telling someone else – a certified coach, for example), *"The story I'm telling myself is…"* and then bring it out in the open. Making the covert overt allows for the opportunity to separate from the story to decide if it's really true.

Once you've brought the story out for what it is, just a story, you have two options:

1. Change it

2. Stop telling it altogether

To change the story, collect new evidence. If collecting new evidence isn't available for you, then create a new story. Choose another way to look at it.

To stop telling the story that has kept you inside your limiting shell, take those automatic wild and story-telling thoughts captive. Catch them, put them on a plane and send them to another land. Catch them, tie an anchor to them and sink them to the bottom of the ocean. Catch them and use the same mind that created them, in an effort to keep you safe in the first place, to creatively send them away.

Once you quiet the busy, busy brain, stress is instantly reduced and you can engage and connect with all your energy – with your whole heart and remarkable mind.

1

For most of my life I told myself the story that I wasn't good enough. In fact, I was born sinful and continually sinned. If you knew me, you'd be surprised I had these thoughts because they didn't show up externally – I didn't have evidence that I was "bad." In fact, I overcompensated externally to prove that I was "good."

I worked really hard to be good. I kept my spaces clean and organized. I did my homework and made good grades, careful to avoid Bs and definitely Cs. In college there were two C scares that required fixing. The first C entailed dropping the class to retake the following semester in order to maintain an academic scholarship. The second C I talked my professor into rounding up, exceptionally up, in order to maintain my scholarship. Being constantly "good" required developing negotiation skills. (I also learned other valuable communication skills. This is to make a point that we continually learn despite any story we're living.)

Arriving to appointments on time was a given, but mostly I'd arrive early. I treated people kindly and didn't speak out much, even on my own behalf, because I didn't want others to see my selfishness. I didn't drink alcohol, and I stayed away from drugs. By external standards I looked like I had a pretty good life, but internally happiness eluded me.

The blemishes on my trying-to-be perfect life record were a few speeding tickets and a couple of fender-benders. To tell you the truth, speeding likely wouldn't stop. For one, the state of harried rushing was just an everyday activity – had to hurry up and meet the expectations of others! Plus, there was an underlying satisfaction in that form of rebellion…because perfection was exhausting and driving fast felt exhilarating.

Over time I began to learn subtle ways to break rules. On one hand I didn't like people telling me what to do and passive-aggressively found ways to get free from the captivity rules made me feel. (I developed an underlying moxie because of this that would serve me later.) On the other hand I felt obligated to try to be good – to make others happy. It was a hard balance to maintain. Down deep, I grew resentful striving so hard when people around me appeared much happier, seemingly without effort.

What that perfection thinking led to was a systematic labeling – a weary state of mind where I had to decide what was "good" and what was "bad" and then make sure to do only good and stay away from anything bad. I was constantly labeling and judging so I could avoid the dark side. If you're a "Star Wars" fan, I had to *earn* The Force. I didn't know that I was already part of it before I was born and that just the simple fact that I was alive and breathing meant I was good…not to mention amazing and beautiful and significant!

Most of my friends had this underlying belief, too. As kids, we were exposed to beliefs that taught us that there were some things in life you didn't do. And if you did do them, you were bad. The thing was, I still felt bad even if I didn't do them.

My story held me captive.

It kept me in constant judgment of myself, and I could only make up for that judgment in external ways. Trying hard to love people was an added frustration because it was something I was "supposed" to do, but most of the time I couldn't muster that either. Tiring, huh?

I remember the day I decided to let it go.

While sitting on my living room couch, I told the God whom I believed created me (but was continually disappointed in me) that I needed a break. I told Him that I was going to lay Him down for a while and see what life is like apart from what I believed about Him. I knew He would still love me as I began to push the envelope, but I had to see for myself. I began to do things I thought I shouldn't do and then I'd pause and wait for lightning to strike or for the world to crash down around me. But that never happened. I learned there is a difference between knowing *about* God and knowing God. Over the course of about twelve months I realized that my story, even though it accidently became my story, was not true.

I was not bad. I was not unworthy of love or goodness. The judgment I continually sensed looming overhead was my own. There was nothing I had to earn. The world didn't have to be a difficult or "bad" place. I wasn't full of sin and neither was anybody else.

I changed my story.

Intelligence did not create me (or you) and then realize there was a mistake. Love knits all Life to sacred wombs, and if that is so then our core contains goodness, not to mention mercy, joy, love, power, and peace. And there's nothing bad about that!

Reconciliation for "evil" took place. I replaced compassion for finger pointing and grace for misunderstanding. "Hmm...," I'd think, "...they just don't know Who they are." I decided that darkness isn't the real problem – lack of light is the problem!

When identification with the shell exists, many people get trapped in "this is it" thinking. As I began to study work that expanded my view of what was real in this world and what was illusion, one of my favorite quotes became my new pair of glasses that looked beyond "this is it" thinking: *Everything is not as it seems. The light at the end of the tunnel is not an illusion. The tunnel is.*

I came across information that the Latin root for the word "perfect" does not mean "without flaws." The word origin and history offers another meaning: "finished."[2] When that one Scripture I'd highlighted as a kid haunts me, I now understand, "Be finished, Rach. God doesn't have to try to be God. He just is. So are you." I AM. Finished.

With new insight, I began to look at myself differently. When inner shift happens, looking at everybody else differently naturally occurs.

A phone call with a friend during this "letting go" gave me space to process this story. He didn't judge me as I worked out my thoughts. In fact, at the end of the call he said, "Rachel, you are good." My first thought was, "No, I'm not" – and I think I even said it out loud – but he came back again with, "You're good." Those words breathed life into me. I believed them. *This was the first crack of the external shell that contained the Great Truth.* In that moment, the old story lost its grip, and a new one began to emerge.

Be aware of the story you've been telling yourself your whole life. Be aware of the story you began telling yourself yesterday. It doesn't matter when it started, it only matters that you become aware of it, separate yourself from it, and decide whether it's really true.

The evolution into your Greatest Self depends on it.

Study Chapter One

Overview/Key Ideas:

- Stories are made up in our minds and are based on our experiences, values, and conditioned thoughts. These stories impact the way we live our lives.
- It is important to have high awareness of how your story is impacting your energy.
- Whatever you believe, you will find evidence to support it.
- When we don't have the whole truth to a situation, our brain automatically fills in the gaps, leaving room for untruth.

Discussion Questions:

- As you read Chapter 1, what stood out to you and why?

- What is a story you are telling yourself?

- What impact is your story having on your satisfaction?

- How true is your story?

- What strategies can you use to change your story or stop the current story?

- What stories have you had recently that have impacted your energy? (Refer to last paragraph on Page 6.)

- Think of something causing you stress.
    - What are the thoughts going on in your mind about the situation?
    - What emotions are evoked?
    - How is your language perpetuating your story?
- How are relationships and culture impacted when individuals experience the same event yet develop different perspectives?
- What story is prevalent in your work culture? How does the story impact the professional environment?

INspired Action

- Think of a story that has recently held you back. List the details that are evidence to your story. What might be a different story you can tell yourself? How might this new story impact your emotions and actions moving forward?

Chapter 2

Detached Involvement

You are not responsible for someone else's happiness.

Detached involvement is a skill everyone needs to know. This one skill directly relates to the effectiveness of engagement and connection in relationships. This skill is a game changer for every aspect of your life, personal and professional.

So what is detached involvement? It means being fully engaged in relationship without taking on the emotions of another. It means being engaged with a distressed person as he or she experiences anger, frustration, sadness, guilt, or grief while not losing oneself in the throes of emotion as well.

My 7-year-old daughter is extraordinarily bright. After a talk with her about friendships one evening, I realized she was not living authentically because she was concerned how others would feel.

"Honey, you're not responsible for someone else's happiness," I assured her.

"But Mom, it feels like I'm supposed to…and it's going to be really hard not to."

A first-grader experiences what most people of all ages experience – a desire to connect in friendship and relationship. However, most people also feel like that means taking on the challenges (or successes) of others to really feel connected.

This is most noticeable when a person who is generally a very giving and loving individual has an encounter with another who sought him or her out to complain or express hurt. There is an underlying message that if someone comes to us in pain, then somehow it is our responsibility to "fix" that pain. Learning to listen while staying out of another's story is what is best for you both.

By practicing detached involvement, an individual continues to give support while still distributing constructive and growth-oriented energy. This is better for all parties in the long run.

If friends fall into a giant pit and can't get out, how helpful is it to jump down into the pit with them? You may keep them company so they're not alone, but now you're all stuck in that dark place. For one to help another, one must maintain a totally different viewpoint – up and around in awareness.

Over time, a lack of detached involvement will create physical and emotional burnout for many leaders. What begins as a way to alleviate pain in others turns into embitterment that it has inadvertently become their own.

When to practice

Here are a couple things to remember when practicing detached involvement.

1. Recognize when your feelings are being affected by another person's story.

You *don't have to* identify and jump into the story, too. You can't "fix" misery or disheartenment by joining in with it. In other words, stay out of the hole! By remaining neutral, you're allowing another to vent so he or she is able to move forward. (Or while in success, remaining neutral gives another the chance to stay in the moment and truly experience the fullness of happiness. Detached involvement allows others to fully have "their moment" without someone else trying to share the attention.)

2. Recognize that you care enough to stay out of another person's story.

Let the successful celebrate! And let the frustrated or hurt or angry feel that way, too! You really can't "save" someone, and jumping in with your own miserable story will not alleviate pain either. While it feels that we're bearing another burden, often both parties walk away just carrying a burden – and no pain has truly been alleviated. When you care deeply, you'll remain in a state of awareness that will inevitably give another the chance to rise above, too.

Providing space is love

The difference between detached involvement and emotional detachment is love. It is out of love that detached involvement is intentional: *Because I love you, I'm going to give you the space to feel exactly how you feel.* Conversely, emotional detachment is done out of lack of love: *I don't really care how you feel. I'm indifferent.*

No matter how backward it may feel, allowing another person space to go through catabolic emotions is one of the best ways for growth. Bringing that awareness into a situation is bringing love into a situation. Love is tuned into the energy of the story but not necessarily the story itself.

The most difficult place to practice this skill is with family. This is also the best place to practice. There is a vested interest in those we do life with intimately, so removing our own ego from the story can take intense present awareness…especially if you've heard the same story for years.

What it looks like

For the most effective use of this skill, stay neutral. Keep your focus on the other person and intently listen without any mental commentary. That means no judgment and no thought about what the person is saying. Allow the story to unfold and provide a loving space for it to be released. Don't pick it up. Don't jump in the box. Allow the story's energy to disperse and watch the person begin to shift when there is no one adding fuel to the sadness or anger, for example.

To be clear, this isn't to be confused with not taking action when action is needed. There is a difference between not being responsible for others' happiness by allowing them space to process, and withholding good from those who genuinely need it. Detached involvement is not withholding. On the contrary, it is holding. It is holding conscious space for others to go through whatever they're going through at that moment. It is allowing what is happening to happen.

Staying out of another's story keeps your own energy from perpetuating it. Giving another space to work out his or her own story is really allowing room to create a new one. Even a 7-year-old can experience the freedom and confident leadership that comes with not feeling the responsibility for anyone else's happiness.

Non-attachment to the outcome

Normally when approached with a story, help often comes in the form of advice or suggestions. When the storytelling is over and people part ways, there can be an attachment made by the "helper" for the help they give to come to fruition in the life of another. This must not be.

If there is attachment to the outcome of the story, an expectation is put into place and the energy between people will not be clear. To be a superlative leader, the outcome has to be given up. It is up to the person living his or her story to write a new chapter and live it out. You can't write the chapter for others and then be attached to that ending. It is not up to you. If non-attachment to the outcome is not practiced, frustration or anger or bitterness are often the result.

This can be best understood with money. If the goal (the outcome) is to make a lot of money, then every encounter to earn that money becomes a means to an end. If there is no attachment to the outcome, then the process itself is what makes you rich!

Not only can attachment to the outcome of a story occur but also the attachment to the success of others. Attachment to others' success is normal because either we truly want others to succeed, or our roles (or jobs) are riding on it. This can be very draining. Teachers may be attached to the success of their students, parents may be attached to the success of their children, bosses to their employees, nurses to their patients. When a bit of our worth or significance is tied into the outcome of another, detached involvement must be consciously practiced to avoid the ups and downs or pressures that oftentimes may be out of our control.

Your own happiness

This concept is not complete without also mentioning that no one else is responsible for your happiness. Putting an expectation on another person (which is usually done unconsciously) to fulfill you, make you happy, make you feel safe, loved or valued is a recipe for suffering for all involved. This is most seen in marriages or intimate relationships and is also a major cause of fallouts in those relationships.

When people enter a relationship talking about their "other half," a little flag raises inside me. When we are looking for our other half, we haven't realized our own wholeness. If wanting to feel loved is the reason for pursuing a relationship, rethink it for a minute. If *you* are not loving your whole self, it doesn't matter who you are in a relationship with, the hole in your half-self will turn into a vacuum and start sucking the life out of another. This is not to say it happens in all relationships, but for many it does. When our wholeness relies on getting our other halfness from someone else, happiness is attached to something external instead of bubbling up from within.

The work of INspired Leadership is to be whole withIN. Once that vast and amazing world has been consciously uncovered, what we create in our external world will deeply impact others.

Detached involvement, along with love and non-attachment to the outcome, will preserve your own energy and serve others in a profound way. The evolution of others can be sped up by encountering loving detached involvement that you provide from a place of wholeness by simply being intensely and totally present.

Recounted via Interview with a Friend – This is his perspective.

I resigned from my leadership position in an organization I loved. At the time the decision felt like the right thing to do, and although I have no regrets about the decision I made, over time it began to look less and less logical – especially to my wife.

I didn't have another job in place when I resigned. We were still paying on our home and nothing about our monthly bills had changed. While my heart assured me the decision was a good one, my mind was subtly telling me at times something different…and so was my wife.

At first, I wanted to fix this uncertainty that settled in our minds. I jumped into my wife's story of frustration about possibly having to sell our home. I tried to help by telling her, "We're gonna be ok" and saying what I could to give her confidence that we'd be fine. She wasn't fully buying it. Her faith in the situation was lacking as she faced the external things that would be changing if I didn't find another job in our area – which wasn't looking that hopeful.

After several months of trying to "help" my wife, I finally realized that I wasn't sure how her needs were going to be met. What I *was* sure about, however, was that it wasn't going to be me who met them. I took a step back. All I could do was detach my involvement in the situation because I knew I didn't have all the answers. I didn't have them for myself, and I certainly didn't have them for her. Her answers were going to have to come from somewhere else.

What I want to be clear about is that doing this, detached involvement, doesn't mean you don't care about the other person. It's done purposefully because of love.

I let my wife wrestle with her own responses to our situation. I loved her during her struggle and gave her space to go through the process she was going through. I didn't bring up our situation all of the time. I worked hard to not show my stress when I paid bills or when we talked about money. By doing this I kept protecting the space she needed to sort everything out. I gave up what that would look like and allowed her to find her own path through it.

This didn't mean I stopped interacting with her. In fact, my interaction with her increased when I gave her the space and let go of the outcome. I became more present in our conversation. Instead of being defensive about my decision or trying to be a problem solver, I engaged her with compassion.

When I let go of trying to solve the problem for my wife, I also let go of the catabolic energy around the issue. This energy was draining me daily. Once I gave up owning how this would be solved, I reached for a higher anabolic energy. I call it faith. To say that I simply turned it over to God isn't enough because of the reality that stared me in the face every day. The first step was letting it go, but the other half of this step was to actually believe it would come true. This isn't to say I had my moments of reverting back to the disbelief, but every time those feelings came up I used strategies to come back to the belief. These strategies came in the form of meditating on this belief, writing it out, saying it out loud, and focusing on Scriptures that proved God stood on His promises.

I also couldn't have done this without a coach. A coach gave me the space to be free about my emotions around this topic. This really helped me from always sharing these catabolic feelings with my wife and reinforced my ability to give her space.

Another pivotal action in moving forward was for me to get real with myself and accept that I stepped down from my position. I took responsibility for my actions and the situation affecting my family and me. This was valuable in helping me move forward. I used no judgment on myself when I accepted it. I used no judgment on myself when my wife was struggling. I told myself the situation "is what it is" and I stopped holding onto my attachment to the outcome. Ironically, this actually got me moving toward a more conscious outcome. The most beautiful part about this process was that I didn't have to come up with the solution for my situation.

By not trying to jump in to "save" us from the situation, my faith was reinforced. I believed God would help my wife through this time far better than I ever could. When I let go, that's exactly what happened.

A month later she attended a women's conference and received a prophetic word that changed the course of her internal struggle. During a segment of the conference when the speaker asked for anyone wanting prophecy to move forward, my wife took action. She got up from her chair and proceeded forward. As she approached the front, the speaker moved over to her and immediately said, "What you are going through isn't the end…it's merely the start. And when you come through it, you will be out into the Promised Land!" This spoke directly to my wife's spirit, leaving her speechless. At the next break, she immediately called me and I sensed the freedom in her voice from then on.

As I shared this story with a men's study I attend, this resonated with them more than anything I was sharing about the situation. I think it resonated because as men, generally we're trying to "fix it" for our wife and children. There is a knight in shining armor persona some men want to uphold to care for their family. In my situation, I just couldn't do it. In fact, the knight in shining armor actually caused some of the frustration in the first place.

I had to give that up. I did it by practicing detached involvement. Even though we were in the same situation, my wife had to be the author of her own story.

Study Chapter Two

Overview/Key Ideas:

- Individuals are responsible for their own happiness.
- When you provide non-judgmental space for others, you care enough to stay out of their story.
- Practicing detached involvement allows individuals to appreciate the journey and not determine success only by the outcome.
- Detached involvement preserves your energy and increases engagement.

Discussion Questions:

- As you read chapter two, what stood out to you and why?

- What does staying "neutral" mean to you? (Refer to page 18.) What does it look like? What behaviors will you see?

- The work of INL is to be whole withIN. Once that has been established, what we create externally will impact others. (Refer to page 21.) What does it mean to be whole withIN?

- Share a time when your feelings were affected by another person's story. How did it affect your energy?

- What does "jumping into someone's box" look like for you? Why is it important to stay out of the box and consciously choose not to be the fixer?

- When this happens at work, what impact does it have on the environment?

• How is practicing detached involvement and emotional detachment an act of love?

INspired Action

• Detached involvement is not withholding. On the contrary, it is holding conscious space for another person to go through whatever they're going through at that moment. During the next encounter with someone, practice holding space for him or her without mental commentary. (Refer to page 18 ~ What it Looks Like.) Reflect on how the experience was different for you and them.

Chapter 3

Judgment

Be curious, not judgmental.

– Walt Whitman

Inside most (if not all) human beings is an inherent desire to belong. In an effort to feel a sense of belonging, human beings have introduced labels. Basically we call things things. These labels help us to better organize and file information that tells us who we are and how the world works.

Where this concept begins to unravel is when we decide whether these labels are "good or bad" or "right or wrong." There's a term for this: judgment. We make a determination, or judgment, about whether this labeled thing is something we like or agree with.

If we agree, then we sense belonging! We're surrounded by hoards of others who believe the same way! "I see you!" they say. And if we've judged the label as "bad" or "wrong," then we reject and resist because it threatens our sense of self and our perception of the world in which we live and interact.

This is the name of most of the world's game: compare and compete.

Who's right, who's wrong. Who matters, who's expendable.

Take politics.

Take sports.

Take religion.

There are plenty of sides to take. Thus plenty of identities are found in determining whose side is "good," "better," or "right." We rally together, wear the same color, sing the same chant, celebrate with thousands when "we" win and find understanding and comfort with thousands when "we" lose. There becomes identification with each other through this lens. These institutions generate millions of dollars and millions of people who reinforce and support our view of ourselves and our view of the world. We find reinforcement that we're on the "right" team and might even find ourselves:

- Labeling a giant franchise "mine": *My (insert team mascot here) won!*
- Claiming sole possession of a deity: *My God is good!*
- Affiliating with a specific political party, which probably doesn't even need this sentence to make the point of taking sides.

Likewise, because of the game we have been taught to play, we find justification that those on the other team (the one that doesn't stroke our identity or beliefs) are "wrong." And we hate it. Maybe it reminds us of the feeling of being alone or insignificant. Maybe our focus is purely idolized. Whatever the reason, there becomes a constant "other" to battle.

When we stop trying to find ourselves in labels, we realize there actually is no self. We see our neighbor *is* our self and loving Self creates instant belonging. Solid communion. Unbreakable connectedness. There is one collective "label." All other labels reduce energy because they are self serving.

Not all people compete. Some don't see competition as necessary, which ironically has potential to create more animosity from those who must see a loser to strengthen their need to be a winner. Rising above comparing and competing allows for room to see that there is enough of everything for everybody. There is enough gratitude, success, and happiness for all – the collective Self. Welcoming these attributes instead of competing for them creates space for the realization of their abundance.

Dropping labels

You belong and are connected more than you probably recognize. By dropping labels, judgments, roles, and identification with institutions, the recognition becomes more prominent. When you do recognize belonging, you will learn the futility of making separation between "us" and "them."

Naturally most of us react in the heat of a moment when someone else is playing the "us versus them" game, particularly when we sense we're the "them." Recognizing when this is happening and not reacting with the same energy is what is called awareness, an awakening, or an increase in consciousness. When existing in this greatness, an inspiring approach to life is present and "the game" becomes null and void. When there isn't an opposing force, the original label-maker will either experience a mutual greatness or will move on to find a new opposing force to reinforce the sense of belonging. Remember that some people need to feel they belong (or are right or important) even if it comes at a cost.

When you come to the soul-gripping, life-changing realization that there is only a collective Us, you can look at human beings as human beings…together…on the same planet…breathing the same air in our lungs, and feeling the same earth under our feet. We can see our Self in another.

Spiritual leaders teach this.

I like something the Buddha said: "See yourself in others. Then whom can you hurt? What harm can you do?"

Jesus teaches this unitary concept, too, when stating that those who say they love God will also love others. He asks how it is possible to love God whom they have not seen, yet hate the people they do see.[1]

Hold up a mirror for people that says *I love you* and *you are me*. And furthermore, *I'm you*.

Experiencing relationship without attaching labels is freeing. The major thing separating or dividing "us" is believing in our minds there is a "them."

Practice non-judgment

To be free from judging your judgments, remember that your brain is doing its job by constantly assessing situations and people as good or bad, right or wrong, urgent or non-urgent by securing surroundings and ensuring survival. However, probably 90% of our judgment doesn't require such life-sustaining discernment anymore.

Most of us are judging by way of opinions, rather than by way of survival. Instead of judging surroundings for predators, we're judging surroundings for comparison. We've exchanged survival for superficial, and our brain is running the show:

That guy is annoying. Her hair is cute. I would never have said that. They don't pay attention to their kids. I'm bored. They don't like me. That dress must've been expensive. They talk so loud on the phone. I can't believe someone posted that. Oh, he is so smart. Oh, he is an ass. I'm out of shape, too fat, too old, too young. And on and on the judgmental chatter goes.

Non-judgment creates silence in your mind. Silence makes room for peace, composure, creativity, really hearing what others are saying, and experiencing life as it unfolds instead of resisting or controlling it.

A quick shift in effective leadership of yourself and others includes practicing non-judgment. Here are some simple ways to be intentional to incorporate non-judgment:

1. Don't judge yourself

Start within you. Your outer world is a direct reflection of your inner world. The most judgmental people are just as judgmental of themselves, and likewise the most accepting of others are self-accepting. Decide to be aware of yourself without constant evaluation and practice self-compassion. Once you've mastered this, a critical spirit will cease to exist within you and in turn will not be directed at others either.

2. "For (insert time frame), I won't judge anything."

Start with half an hour, for example. Experience the half hour without an opinion. Be mindful of your thoughts. You can work up to two hours, a particular event, or eventually try a full day.

3. Accept each moment

Experience the moment as it unfolds and accept it. Go with the flow of Life and be conscious to accept who you are with, what you are doing, and where you are. Resisting *what is* is an indication we have judged the moment.

It may feel irresponsible at first, but work on experiencing the moment without judging or resisting it. One way to think of this is, "Say yes to life." Continually say yes to each moment. This is a great practice while sitting at a stoplight, waiting in line, or being served by what you have determined is a slow waitress, for example.

4. Separate opinions from facts

Determine what are facts versus opinions based on your perception in the moment at hand. Practice seeing situations as they are by being open and curious.

5. Be curious

When you do feel yourself heading down the critical road, take a step back and be curious. First, begin with curiosity for yourself about why you're upset. *Wow…why does that bother me so much?*

With others, be curious about another person's choice before judging it. Be open to situations you would normally dislike and be curious about what opportunity is there. Curiosity provides space and composure to meaningfully connect in the moment.

6. Learn to use discernment

Discernment is a task of the spirit. Judgment is a task of the mind. Quiet your mind to *know* in a different way.

Non-judgment will revolutionize your world – first your inner world and then immediately the world around you. Substituting judgment with curiosity is one small shift in your thinking that will create subsequent enormous shifts to follow.

When you go out in the woods and look at trees, you see all these different trees. And some of them are bent, and some of them are straight, and some of them are evergreens, and some of them are whatever. And you look at the tree and you allow it. You see why it is the way it is. You sort of understand that it didn't get enough light, so it turned that way. And you don't get all emotional about it. You just allow it. You appreciate the tree. The minute you get near humans, you lose all that. And you're constantly saying 'You're too this, or I'm too this.' That judging mind comes in. And so I practice turning people into trees. Which means appreciating them just the way they are.
– Ram Dass

Recounted via Interview with a Friend – This is his perspective.

One of the biggest shifts in my life came when I stopped judging. I made this shift intentionally because I was just tired of it. I was tired of the catabolic energy that judging myself all the time was creating. Once I removed the judgment of myself, I stopped judging others. This allowed me to love myself and then really love others.

I noticed when I didn't put a label on people, I could really see them for who they were!

The event that led to my conscious decision to remove judgment from my life coincidentally began at church. I was asked to serve on my church board and during the interview they asked me whether I could uphold certain criteria to serve. First, I was asked to speak truthfully, which wasn't a problem for me. Second, I was told I could not drink alcohol. Instantly my thought was, "Jesus loves me if I want to have a drink or not." Although I left alcohol out of my life many years before and this criteria was not an issue, I left that meeting with a big eye-opener. I felt judgment, that somehow drinking alcohol would exclude me from something I was very capable of doing.

None of the gentlemen on the board made me feel this way, I want to be clear about that, but I walked out feeling that at times in my life I made others feel the way I felt during that meeting, and I realized at points in my life I had contributed to that message. I had an aha moment that I'd been doing that in my life. I did it in my profession. The way I carried myself came across as condescending. Walking out of that meeting brought all this to head and it bothered me. It's important to me how I make people feel, and if I made people feel that I was somehow more righteous than them, then it had to stop!

During this new journey without judgment, the first place I began was my values – I left them out of my encounters with people. Before, if the values of others didn't align with mine, I'd stick an imaginary badge on them and label them. I'd treat them by the way I labeled them, and unfortunately a lot of those labels read "bad."

People pick up on judgment, you know…in body language, in tone, and in compassion. They sense that. When I interact now, I'm intentional to be curious and find out more about them. I keep a neutral expression, and I feel love for the person. In no way do I want them to feel any "less" because of me.

Self-righteousness is really a good indication of judgment. I carried it much of my life and let off a condescending energy. I never want anyone to feel that way again.

While I did serve on the board, I stepped down within two months. It had to do more with time than with the criteria, but I did learn one of the most valuable lessons that day.

Shortly after this epiphany, I extinguished whatever self-righteousness was left within me on a vacation with my family. I intentionally ordered a Mai-Tai while on the beach, and I was very conscious to enjoy it while simultaneously enjoying the presence of the God who created me. My 24-year-old daughter even said, "Dad!" and I knew as I ordered the drink, and another one that followed, that I was also releasing that religious spirit from her as I explained why I ordered and enjoyed the drinks.

Judgment can look like body image, income, perfectionism, parenting style, projection of expectations on others, work ethic, use of language, political views, and so on. Whatever you can release in yourself, do it. Practice self-acceptance and self-compassion; they are the opposite of judgment.

When I was free from judgment of myself, I was free to *really* love others.

Study Chapter Three

Overview/Key Ideas:

- Placing labels on people or situations creates limitations and separation.
- Practicing non-judgment makes room for peace, composure, creativity, and hearing what others are saying.
- Rising above comparing and competing allows for room to see that there is enough gratitude, success, and happiness for all.
- Curiosity provides an opportunity for meaningful connection.

Discussion Questions:

- As you read Chapter 3, what stood out to you and why?

- What labels do you use or see used from a place of judgment?

- How are your judgments of self and others impacting your satisfaction?

- How does silencing mental judgment make room for hearing what others are really saying?

- In what ways do you judge yourself? How would giving yourself more acceptance and compassion impact you?

- How would replacing judgment with curiosity shift engagement and connection with others?

- How is judgment impacting your professional environment?

INspired Action

- Most of us judge through opinions rather than by way of survival. We've exchanged survival for superficial, and our brains are running the show. (Refer to page 31 – Practicing Non-Judgment.)
    - Cultivate curiosity. During a conversation, practice asking curious questions. Set aside any preconceived ideas or thoughts of what should happen or what needs to happen and just be curious.
    - Decide on a time frame (an hour, a day, a week, etc). Be conscious of the judgments you make. Determine if these judgments are connected to a value and how it might benefit you to release these judgments.

Chapter 4

Rewrite Your Rules

May your choices reflect your hope and not your fears.

– Nelson Mandela

Values drive us. They are the unseen and sometimes unrealized driving force behind our actions. When values are examined and prioritized, it becomes very clear why we react certain ways and how we can choose our action more consciously.

Exploring your values benefits everything you do. If something you value is threatened, you get upset. If something you value is being expressed or honored, life will feel really good.

It will not take long to realize why you're feeling upset or why you're feeling great, and this is key in increasing awareness, which is key in increasing satisfaction in life.

Rules

In addition to exploring values, the exploration of the rules by which you live creates greater awareness.

Everyone has a set of rules. The rules were either put upon you by the expectations and rules of others, or you created them yourself by consciously or unconsciously assessing what values are most important. However they came to exist, a strict adherence to them can greatly limit your action or unconsciously drive your action. If necessary, breaking your own rules can help you stop being defined by them, and you will find yourself free to explore and discover more of who you really are.

Uncovering a rule

While coaching a powerful, goal-setting woman, a topic naturally continued to come up around competition and hard work. One of her life rules surfaced during a conversation surrounding a 5K with friends. She was bent on winning while her friends were only hoping to finish. She wanted to kick the race's ass or have a personal best at the least, so she was frustrated from the start. The unconscious rule that surfaced was *Failure is not an option*. To this already amazing woman, second place was the first loser and to avoid failing during the race, she must work as hard as possible to prove herself a winner.

By the end of our time, she added to her on-going list of old rules and planned to rewrite the option of failure to alleviate frustration and allow freedom in many areas of life. Not only did she uncover the unconscious rule but she reflected that had she been fully present with her friends instead of attached to the outcome of the race, she would have enjoyed the experience even more.

(When typing this chapter I checked back to ask about her rule word for word. She texted me the old rule followed by another text: *Haha!!!* When we realize the rules we've been unconsciously holding ourselves to, humor seems like the best logical response!)

How to uncover your own rules

To uncover your rules, be very conscious about two things:

1. When are you upset?

2. When does life seem to be smooth and enjoyable?

Be aware in these moments to be curious, and start making a running list of rules as they surface. (Don't get hung up on the word "rules." It's just a label to help you become aware of what expectations may be driving your action or inaction.) Here are some examples of rules:

- Succeed at all costs
- Authority is not to be fully trusted
- I need to prove my worth
- Keep a spotless home and yard
- Conflict is to be avoided
- Showing emotion is weak
- Money makes me important
- My kids are a reflection of me

When your life experience is not something that brings you love, peace, or joy, ask yourself what rule you are trying to follow. Where did that rule come from? What happens if you break that rule? How is it limiting you? Then begin to decide how you *really* want to live.

The time for this naturally emerges during transitions in life. For example, a new job, marriage, having children, the death of a spouse, or retirement are big transitions. Richard Rohr, author of *Falling Upward*, calls the point in life where everything up to that point suddenly needs adjusting as "the second half of life."[1] The first half of life we're building our kingdoms, probably living by rules that get us ahead or lead to success or just seem like the next thing to do on the checklist of life. The second half of life begins with a deep shift in perspective followed by redefining who you are. Transition has the potential to naturally turn us 180 degrees, and our old ways begin to look differently, perhaps even way off. Wayne Dyer calls this "the afternoon." By the time you get to the afternoon, most of the things you knew that morning aren't true!

Being the author of how you want to live puts you at the keyboard – typing, deleting, and editing until who you are aligns with what you're choosing.

It may be uncomfortable at first to challenge the way you've always "done life." It may be uncomfortable to let some of those rules go that feel so imperative to uphold. It may be uncomfortable to experience the reactions of others who are uncomfortable with your "new self." Knowing this discomfort may occur is the first step in accepting and moving through it as you begin to decide new rules by which you want to play the game of life. On the other hand, if a transition has led to an automatic shift in thinking, then making the changes may come more easily.

To give you some examples, here are a few of my conscious rules. As my values changed, so did my rules:

- People are inherently good, find it
- Others may benefit by what I say, speak up
- Accept people right where they are
- Live in the Now
- Share my gifts, unafraid
- Live with passion and enthusiasm

Try this process to uncover your values and discover your rules. Challenge the rules and determine which ones aren't working anymore. Get really conscious about what you want to experience in life and give yourself permission to let those old rules go.

When you recognize when conditioned old-rule mindsets or emotions are triggered, try saying out loud, "That is the way I *used* to think. Now, I think *this (fill in the blank)*." This can be an easy way to begin to separate from the old rule thinking and make space for the real You, without limitations or expectations, to emerge.

1

    I met Greg in the mountains one day after a blizzard. I'd actually first met him in the exact location two years earlier. I wouldn't have been able to pick him out of a crowd, but as soon as I began to experience his relaxed nature and genuine likability, I thought to myself, *that's that guy...*

    Appearances aren't always recognizable but vibes always are. I remembered his vibes and still found him interesting two years later. I found his tattoos interesting, too.

    I couldn't help my curiosity while studying the ski instructor's hands as he checked our kids into ski school. The clearly visible tattoos were sets of numbers and a letter across four knuckles on each hand, and I would spot an occasional roundish tattoo play peek-a-boo from under the end of his shirt sleeve.

    As we passed paperwork back and forth, I enjoyed our exchange. His laid-back demeanor gave the stress of our blizzard-induced late arrival less attention (we intended to be there 18 hours earlier), and he instantly calmed my embarrassment of checking in six kids with three minutes to spare and two sets of ski goggles still missing.

    My first inclination was genuine fondness toward this man, and my second was genuine curiosity about the numbers and letters forever inked into his skin. That afternoon, after spotting him instructing two of my friend's kids down one of the ski runs, I had a chance to ask him about it.

"Oh, I love this," he told me as he rubbed his hands together. "I umpire Little League in the summer. In the rulebook, according to Rule 901C, the umpire has the authority to rule on anything not specifically mentioned in the rulebook. And 902A says that an umpire's judgment calls are not allowed to be argued, and if someone does they become subject to ejection."

He then held out one inked fist, "so I get to make the rules," and then he held up the other fist, "and you can't tell me what to do."

Immediately my connection to this man was sealed. In my own life oftentimes I feel an awkwardness in playing the game of life because I don't like some of the rules or I'm not always sure what the rules are in the first place. All I knew at that moment with Greg was that I have a small aversion to people telling me what to do, and I've always been eager to make up my own rules.

I want to be clear that making up your own rules does not have to be an act of rebellion. In the context of this chapter, it is an act of intention. You always have a choice in how you respond to your life experience, and I was curious not only about Greg's attention to life but his intentional response as well.

I pressed further, asking about the other tattoo beneath his shirt sleeve, which represented a significant rock band to him, and then he showed me two more tattoos – one on the inside of each forearm. They were semicolons.

"These represent anti-bullying," he said, "because I was bullied as a kid. This one pointing away represents my promise to my friends and family that I will never view self-harm as an option again, and the one pointing toward me is a promise to myself as well…and to always help those who are in the same helpless situation."

I wanted to talk more with Greg, but he had ski lessons to teach. I tucked our conversation into my heart to ponder later.

Because of the blizzard delaying our trip one day, we were granted an extension at the ski resort an extra day. Because of this "mishap" (I called it a nightmare at the time), I was given the opportunity to bump into Greg again two days later. (This also happened to be the last day the resort was open! I love when things like this happen because I know with deeper conviction that chance meetings are not by chance.) I asked if he would be willing to let me interview him more and use his story in this book. I didn't have to know the story before I knew I would use it – my intuition had already assured me this would be happening.

He graciously accepted, shook my hand, and a few days later I called him. Below is the gist of what I heard in as close to Greg's voice as possible.

…

I learned about 901C and 902A during the time when I was being bullied in school. My dad, who also umpired, was reading the rulebook out loud and joked about those rules being cool tattoos. Eight years later is when I got the tattoos.

Being bullied is torture.[2] It was beyond confusing, and I couldn't focus on what I wanted to focus on. It took up my whole day, "Oh god, what am I going to walk into? What am I going to walk away with?" You know, at age 14, it was weeks of straight hell at school.

I was so confused as a kid why I was a target. In elementary school I'd just won the spelling bee, I was smart, I played hockey, was the first baseman in baseball, I played football and soccer…I was a great athlete. Elementary school was awesome, but then middle school is when everything started. Bullying, to me, was verbal abuse – kids saying messed up stuff, not giving me a chance to breathe or be alone. It's like constantly having a mosquito that wants to come back and come back, bagging and going on…it's so destructive.

I think the most damaging thing was that it made me realize that not everybody out there is going to help. I became really distrusting. I questioned everything – people I trust and love. Those people never gave me a reason to question them before, but I was constantly leary about the people I was around. This was not how I wanted to view people. This was not who I wanted to be.

I got into alcohol and smoking and drugs at 14. I hated who I was, you know, not because of who I was…but because of these people. I thought I was a pretty great person, so I was confused. I'd heard "great job" up to this point in my life, in school and on the field, but then was ridiculed every single day.

I thought, "What am I doing wrong?" The bullying was mostly verbal assaults. One I'll never forget was when a guy told me, "Yeah, your girlfriend's hair looks like a crap I took this morning." I mean, I can laugh about it now, but at the time I didn't understand. I wondered *what have I done to deserve to any of this? What was so wrong with me that I became a target?* So I basically said "screw it" and turned to coping and numbing with alcohol and drugs.

My parents were like, "This isn't Greg. What's going on?" I told them that I didn't feel safe at school. I didn't want to go to school. I did not want to go back there. I did not want to do this. I broke down because I couldn't cope with the fact people didn't like me because of who I am, but I think I'm an OK person. I went from an academic athlete to drug-using rebel. I finally told my parents about what I was doing.

My dad's reaction was, "I wish you'd never gotten that bass guitar." When he said that, I thought that even my dad doesn't want me to do things I enjoy. That bass was my escape from a really messed up reality and it made a big impact on my life. Since being 5 years old I remember loving music, and when I got that bass it's like it awakened something powerful inside of me.

I waited for my parents to go to bed that night and took that bass outside (the thing that kept me sane at this point) and smashed it into pieces. I shattered it. After that, I felt the calm of complete despair. When so many things turn you sideways that you're beyond angry or sad, you stop feeling. It's a scary calm. There's no anger, no hatred. I thought that I don't want this life anymore; it's not OK with me.

I was so calm when I went into the kitchen and got a knife and put it to my throat. I'm not religious or anything, but I have to believe in guardian angels because right as my muscles tensed up, it felt like someone came up behind me with headphones and put them on my ears and I heard music. The music played over and over again and it made me stop. The music shocked me into reality and I realized what I was doing and dropped the knife. My dad came around the corner and almost saw his son with his throat wide open.

Not knowing what to do when being bullied is the worst. It could lead to violence or revenge. The rules on my knuckles tie into this because I started to learn that no matter what the bullies did, I was the one who controlled what happened to me. It was my reaction and what I read in the situation that truly affected me. Even though they were doing all these things, I was technically the one making the rules.

Eventually the bullying lit a fire under me. I realized that it had more to do with them than with me. When I got out of school, I got to choose the people I wanted to be around and my eyes opened. A handful of guys spent so much time to come and mess with me…so much time and effort was made to ruin my day. Think about what they could have done if they'd have put that time and effort into something else.

...

I asked Greg if he had a platform in which to share something, what would he want to say. He said this: "Slow down."

And then he paused.

"Slow everything down. Think before you're going to say the things you're going to say. Think before you're going to do something."

He went on to explain to me that if he found the people today who bullied him 10 years ago, he believes they wouldn't be the same people they were then. If they'd slowed down and taken a step back, if they'd thought about their words and actions, they really wouldn't have done it.

He said, "As ski instructor, the thing I hear myself saying the most is, 'Just slow down.' I say it all the time. We get so amped up doing things in life. People charge ahead, gotta get straight As, graduate, then graduate from somewhere else, then find something else. What did you do? You end up being 60 and realize you rushed your entire life away.

"When people fall while skiing, their bodies get tangled up in all kinds of different ways and they scramble to hurry and get up and get twisted up even more. I tell them, 'Slow down.' When you slow down and look at the pieces, it all makes complete sense. This happens in skiing, in careers, relationships…slow down, breathe and think."

My new friend also shared that he considers every day what impact he makes on others.

"Everybody has bad stuff happen," he said. This is why he's conscious to treat people with compassion and respect – he made up his own rules to follow.

When you make your own rules, consider including slowing down, loving others, and considering your impact daily. While your appearance may not be remembered, your vibes will always be remembered because of the way you made someone feel.

I learned this rule from a warm, easygoing, conscientious, intelligent, athletic, tattooed, gnarly snowboarder – and I'll never forget it.

...

On a side note, I want to confess that I've been guilty of poo-pooing bullying. While in the teaching profession, it became an initiative to implement bullying curriculum, but I saw it as something dumped on us rather than explained and trained. Had I heard a testimony from someone like Greg, I'd have taken it more seriously.

While this short excerpt about Greg brings the effects of bullying to light and shares a bit of new rules he created for himself, it is only a small piece of what I got to experience during our full conversation. My definition and idea of bullying has forever been changed, and Greg and I share the bewilderment that human beings can intentionally hurt other human beings. It baffles me. This encounter has increased my capacity for compassion and my wherewithal to step in when I sense dissonance.

Loving people without judgment will evolve the world, and since meeting Greg I'm consciously editing my rules to be as inclusive and wide open as possible.

Greg's tattoos: 901C & 902A

Lovely Day Boutique at etsy.com

When Greg said, "Slow down," I immediately walked over to this painting on my office wall and took a picture and sent it to him. That moment solidified his message in this book for me.

Study Chapter Four

Overview/Key Ideas:

- Values are the unseen and sometimes unrealized driving force behind our actions.
- We consciously and unconsciously hold ourselves and others to certain rules.
- As values change, rules change or even disappear.

Discussion Questions:

- As you read Chapter 4, what stood out to you and why?
- What rules are you living by in your life?
- By what rules are you expecting others to live?
- Share one rule that causes you stress. How might that rule be changed to better serve you?
- When life is going particularly well for you, what values are being honored?
- When life feels hard, chaotic, or frustrating, what values are being neglected, challenged, or disregarded?
- What are some unwritten rules in your organization? How would bringing them out in the open impact your organization?

INspired Action

- When your life experience is not something that brings you love, peace, or joy, ask yourself what rule you are trying to follow. Make a list of rules by which you live and determine which ones aren't working for you anymore. Once you identify which rules are no longer serving you, rewrite them! (Refer to Page 41 – How to uncover your rules.)

Chapter 5

Shhhh…Listen!

Most people do not listen with the intent to understand; they listen with the intent to reply.

— Stephen R. Covey

*L*ook here! Wait – over HERE! Have you considered THIS?! Do you SEE what's HAPPENING?? You DON'T WANT to MISS THIS! And it's ALL TRUE!

We don't have to look far to find bombardment of frenzied breaking news, immediate weighing in of opinion, or even the slightest possibility of risk proposed to our daily life. It seems to be around every corner. What some people don't know is that constantly reacting to every controversial topic only creates more noise.

Shhh…you don't have to weigh in. You do not have to get sucked into the frenzy. You don't have to be scared, either. It's not necessary.

Over the past few years, the value of silence has quietly come forward in the form of three lessons.

Lesson 1: The largest ego seems the loudest.

Egos are projections of who we think we are versus who we really are. They are usually created by labels, expectations, or how we *want* to be portrayed. Egos have to be maintained, so constant work has to be done on the part of the ego to ensure its existence…and importance.

Noise in the form of ego sounds like this: *I think…* or *But wait…* Or there's an underlying message of *Look at me…* or *I'm right…* Ego makes assertions or feels defensive, so it must project itself or defend itself. Whichever way it chooses to make itself known, it has to make noise. The louder it is, the more attention it feels it gets. And the more attention it gets, the more important it feels.

Quiet can be viewed by the ego as weak or insignificant (and you will read in Chapter 9 the ego is afraid of diminishing). However, calm and confidence can be quiet and content.

Confidence does not have to prove anything. It rests within silence and does not feel a need to fill it up.

Silencing the ego is a huge step in awareness. When you recognize a demanding urge to speak up to prove something or defend yourself? Just. Don't. Speak. You don't have to. Therein lies your true power.

Lesson 2: Listening is the best option in any given conversation.

Listening to understand is completely different than listening to reply. Generally people only listen enough to form something to say in response – to generate more noise. But listening intently to truly understand another person is like dropping a bucket down into a deep well and then drawing out fresh, cool water. It's refreshing.

Listen and, in response, clarify what you heard. You will find that bucket will drop again and draw up parts of a person that are beautifully intimate and delicately private. There is a deeper connection available. Quiet can take conversations to depths that noise never can.

The coaching process itself is based on listening. It is sometimes astounding to me that listening alone, without any other coaching skills, can leave people feeling extremely valued and loved. Really being heard and validated may be so uncommon a practice these days that when it does occur, people are open to doing whatever it takes to work through the process of what is truly limiting them. Authenticity then becomes the unbreakable bond between coach and client, husband and wife, or parent and child.

Lesson 3: Unplug from electrical devices and plug into the electrifying life around you.

A starry night has more brilliance than a computer screen. Watching the whisper of wind in the trees creates a calm that a text message cannot touch. Listening to birds sing overhead instills an internal pause like being between songs on your musical playlist.

You've heard it, right? Between songs? Listen, it's silence.

Without silence, we wouldn't notice the noise.

When I was a little girl, my great-grandpa introduced me to the Phoebe bird. I can't pick the bird out of a line-up, but I can recognize its song anywhere. My mom's name is Phoebe, so there is an added layer of amusement when hearing the bird's two-tone song. It goes high-low, high-low as it says *FEE-bee, FEE-bee.* When the song is audible, I instantly become mindful and smile. If my kids are around I immediately call them to attention: "Guys! Did you hear the Phoebe bird?" We stand frozen, with only our eyes moving back and forth to one other, until we hear the *fee-bee* echo from a distant location. We smile to each other, one of us inevitably whistles fee-bee back, and then we stand in silence and wait to hear it again.

Being intensely aware in silence makes noise that much more meaningful.

Practicing silence in a noisy world allows others to experience the internal space that accompanies internal quiet. They will be drawn to you. These people will enrich your life – not compete with it, stifle it, or suffocate it.

You can sit in the company of anyone with a peace that nothing *has* to be said because silence encompasses everything you can't put into words. When we learn to be silent, the overwhelming value presents itself…and the noise and frenzied bombardment won't pull us in or drown out the peace within anymore.

I became aware of my ego and began to disengage from it during a conference phone call with four other people I had not met in person.

In a whirlwind of coincidental connections I found myself collaborating over the phone with two high-profile men and two self-confident women over a shared computer screen, discussing material for a developing business. There were times leading up to that point when I would reflect and offer feedback via email or phone calls, but it was only between me and the men who co-founded the business. I enjoyed the sole attention and conversation. They liked me. They respected me. They appreciated my knack for offering outside-the-box thinking and for providing a space for them to reflect. My feelings and appreciation toward them were mutual. I enjoyed and respected them both. However, I was unaware how my ego was being fed by these encounters until that conference call.

Coincidentally, a large portion of the material and structure of the budding business included training in recognizing that people in general think they need external accomplishment or recognition to feel complete or whole, and then realizing that by continually focusing on the external to meet internal needs, they'd never have enough. In other words, there is nothing that satisfies the ego. It can never get enough.

During the call, I was first put off by some of the small talk, mostly from the women who seemed to be focusing on nothing *but* the external. (I hadn't read Chapter 3 of this book yet. Gulp.) As we progressed through the slides for discussion, I would listen to the feedback from the women and then I'd jump in with my two cents. It hadn't dawned on me at that time, but in hindsight it was very clear I was competing in energy to keep up with the women – I wanted to be heard. I had things to offer! I had some opinions to make known!

It wasn't until halfway through the call when it suddenly struck me that I was not really contributing to be helpful – I was contributing to feel important.

The truth slammed me, and I came face to face with the "ego" I'd been reading about and discussing. I saw that everything I'd heard and read was true, and self-actualization humbled me. This ego was not content – it not only wanted its own way but also recognition and attention. Once I became aware of this phenomenon, one thing was certain: I did not like how it felt when the ego was in command.

As soon as I recognized what was happening, I stopped. I only spoke after discerning the input to be beneficial. I listened to what others were saying and tried to understand their viewpoints instead of competing with them. I understood that their contribution was not taking away from me. I was taking away from myself, my authenticity, by trying so hard to be important.

Nearing the end of the call, one of the men said, "Rachel, you haven't said much, what do you think?" To this question, I replied very intentionally without a motive. I gave my genuine feedback and asked more about what he was thinking, allowing him to reflect.

I found that when I didn't puff up to make a point to be heard, I would either be invited into the conversation when necessary or have greater discernment about the best time to add value. I also learned that if I'm ever trying to be heard by projecting myself, or if I am defensive in any way, this was not me. This was the ego that sabotages the real me.

What cemented this lesson in ego came after our call was over in the form of an email from one of the men. It read, "Thank you for being on the call today. You spoke the least, but you said the most."

From that point on, I understood the power of listening. I understood the power of quiet. I understood that not having to project or defend was freeing, and I consciously stopped doing it. When I recognize the ego rise up (and it will), I don't immediately speak. By waiting for the feeling to subside, I remember who I am, and I let the weight of my words matter instead of the number of them.

The beginning of truly being powerful comes with the awareness of not having to prove you are.

Expanding and growing sometimes means trimming branches. The trees don't compete and compare with one another, they just grow alongside each other. The evolving of something small into something mighty doesn't require more. Sometimes it requires less.

Study Chapter Five

Overview/Key Ideas:

- Silencing the ego is an important step in awareness.
- Listening to understand is different than listening to reply.
- Being heard makes a person feel valued and improves relationships.

Discussion Questions:

- As you read Chapter 5, what stood out to you and why?
- How does your mental agenda impact our ability to listen?
- How comfortable are you with silence?
- What will you be intentional about as you listen to understand?
- How does preoccupied listening get in the way of developing relationships?
- What do you think about the concept of an ego?
- When can being "loud" be necessary and not come from a place of ego?
- What would be different in your organization if people listened to understand?

INspired Action

- Practice silence during your next conversation. Listen intently, clarify what you heard and then ask a curious question. Give the person space to reflect back. Reflect how your engagement in the conversation was different and the impact it had for you, the other person, and the situation.

Chapter 6

The Gift of Intuition

The intuitive mind is a sacred gift and the rational mind is a faithful servant. We have created a society that honors the servant and has forgotten the gift.

– Albert Einstein

Steve Jobs called intuition "more powerful than intellect," and if you've experienced it, you know it is. In fact, intuition surpasses analytical thinking, and intuitive "knowing" becomes something that is hard to describe.

I don't really know it here (point to head)…I just know it here (point to gut).

Intuition is a gut feeling, an instinct, a hunch or a sense. By its very nature it can easily be avoided because 1. It sounds pretty *non*-concrete and 2. When thinking of the sixth sense, "I see dead people" from the 1999 blockbuster movie may come to mind.

According to a leading personality indicator, only 30% of the population favors intuition – what is not seen or spoken – and 70% prefers the sensory option – "what I see is exactly what I get."

Leading yourself and others with intuition means tapping into a power that exceeds thought, which for 70% of the population means accessing something that feels a little unnatural. In intentionally doing so, this leaves room for something greater than yourself, which is to say greater than your initial thoughts, to guide and direct you.

In athletics, intuition can be likened to "the zone." Remember the game that gave you goosebumps? Remember that moment that stands out to you as a player when you weren't thinking but just moving and tuned in and in sync with everything around you? Remember feeling part of something bigger than yourself and it was almost surreal? Maybe you can even recall a feeling of slow motion?

Yea, that's The Zone…Rivers of Living Water…Intuition…we're talking about the same thing.

In business, intuition cultivates creativity or even a "lucky break." In leadership, intuition cultivates stronger relational bonds and a knack for bringing out the best in people. In personal life, intuition cultivates purpose and Oneness and trust about following the map of Life inside. This map gives subtle direction and information about the connectedness of life outside of you. The compass for this map is intuition.

When intuition is in use, there is no agenda. Intuition is neutral and direct. It doesn't come from our own wants or to try to manipulate a situation or person, it comes from a place of awareness.

We have all experienced intuition. Maintaining and staying in the flow of it is where the magic happens.

How to tune into intuition

1. Practice getting quiet

The constant chatter in your mind is the biggest block to accessing intuition. You can't tune in if you are constantly distracted. Practice mindfulness, total focus on the present moment, to get completely engaged and connected to what is happening in and around you.

2. Pay attention to coincidence

Instead of passing off little coincidental instances as "nothing," pay attention. (Remember the blizzard "nightmare" delay that allowed me to run into Greg? And the "Slow Down" painting on my office wall, which was his message when I asked what he'd say if he had a platform?) When you were thinking about someone and the phone rang and it was that person – make a mental note that your intuition was in play. When you made a decision based on a gut feeling and it turned out to be really wise – make a mental note. When a co-worker came to you with a certain story but you disregarded the story entirely and pegged another issue instead – make a mental note. Begin to notice what's "between the lines" and become aware when your intuition raises a flag.

Over time you will begin to recognize that "coincidence" is just the flow of Life and you are part of It. As you become more aware and collect evidence of intuition, your trust of yourself will increase. You will discover that you really do have everything you need inside you, which will remove the pressure to seek and search elsewhere.

This is not to say that seeking wise counsel is out of the question. By all means, get a mentor. Hire a coach. Talk with a pastor. The value of trusting your own intuition, the greatness inside you, empowers you to know that your answers lie within. You learn to pay attention.

In leading yourself and others in the highest possible way, learning to tap into the "knowing" that surpasses thinking is something that will give you an internal edge in a mostly externally functioning world.

As I'm typing this, I recognize that intuition has led me to this exact moment. More than two years ago intuition led me to email a stranger after a *coincidental* phone call to my husband out of the blue at the exact *right* time. Making that contact, which developed into a friendship, proved invaluable as a month later I learned that cancerous cells set up camp in my dad's pancreas. The friendship provided a stake in the ground for me to question Life deeply to make sense of the journey of Dad's existence and seemingly imminent mortality.

It's pure speculation to say *had I not trusted my gut, what would be different,* so the point here is that I did. I went with it. And what unfolded was meaningful.

In one year, from the moment we learned about Dad to the moment we watched him leave his shell, the new friendship created a space to reflect and learn and process, which shifted my internal world at the core.

During that year, I also played a small part in a budding company co-founded by the random email friend and his buddy, whose philosophies felt totally aligned with mine. Digging deep at this stage of development, I learned a little about business and relationships and a lot about myself in relation to those two things. This experience continues to be an influential factor in my contribution to the development of INspired Leadership.

Additionally during this time I found out my teaching certification was up for renewal. It came to my attention that eight hours were required to do this…in four months! I remember, with acceptance, thinking, "Well, that's it. My license is going to expire."

Without much hope, really, I looked up our local service center and scrolled through its list of workshops. (They are .5 credit hours, by the way! The likelihood of me taking 16 of those babies in four months was zilch to none!) Only one workshop stood out. However, it may as well have stood up off the page and slapped me in the face. The title was "Seven Levels of Energy Leadership." To be honest, the leadership part didn't appeal to me, but the energy part did. Since working with the budding business and two amazing businessmen during the past year, the description sounded like ideas in which I'd already been involved. After reading the workshop description, I trusted my gut to sign up even though in the back of my mind I knew the license renewal was physically impossible.

What followed is the reason you're reading this sentence.

At the workshop, after dropping my materials at a table, I approached a woman to talk about my excitement about the workshop. I was excited about buzz words like *energy*, *intuition*, *transcending ego*, *awareness*, *consciousness*, *emotions*, and *judgment*, to name a few. I remember telling her about *non-resistance* and *non-attachment,* among other concepts that spoke to my heart during a difficult time when our family watched our emaciated dad prove the transient nature of life. The concepts fed me (grew my heart capacity) and led me (to this woman at this workshop) because of following a gut instinct to send an email to a man I didn't know.

The woman, it turns out, was equally as excited. Tamara Konrade, the professional learning team lead at the service center (ESSDACK), enthusiastically said to me within two minutes, "I'd hire you right now!" I laughed at the time at the zealous comment, but it turned out to be foreshadowing.

Because of that encounter, I was introduced to coaching and given the opportunity to be trained in Core Energy Coaching. (This "work" absolutely aligned with who I am!) Because of that training, I met people who have not only inspired me but have become intimate friends along this journey.

From a seemingly random phone call, to a cancer diagnosis, to a seemingly shut door to recertify a teaching license, to training in core energy coaching, to an explosion of meaningful encounters, to the moment you're reading these words, the opportunity to write this book was unfolding. Using the gift of intuition led me to connect the dots along the way.

Intuition isn't hocus-pocus. It's flowing in the River of Life. It is recognizing when things happen, as they happen, that what is meant for you will not miss you and what misses you is not meant for you. It is going with the flow while simultaneously being fully aware of it.

I received this notebook during our first INL retreat, clinching my belief that our message would be significant.

Core Energy Coach Training Group

The INL Team (from left to right): Meg Wilson, Tammy Fellers, Tamara Konrade, Rachel Thalmann, Mike Sanders

Study Chapter Six

Overview/Key Ideas:

- Intuition means tapping into a power that exceeds thought.
- Intuition does not have an agenda.
- Intuition is neutral and direct.
- As you become more aware of your intuition, trust of yourself will increase, and you will discover you have everything you need within you.

Discussion Questions:

- As you read Chapter 6, what stood out to you and why?

- What does intuition mean to you?

- When do you follow your intuition? When do you not follow your intuition?

- How would you benefit by allowing yourself to trust your intuition more?

- How might an organization change if intuition was a value?

- How will focus on the present moment help you engage and connect with what is happening in and around you?

INspired Action

- Instead of passing off little coincidental instances as nothing, pay attention. The next time you have a gut instinct or hunch, follow it and see what happens. Reflect on your experience.

Chapter 7

Mindful versus Mind Full

> *Mindfulness: paying attention to the present moment with intention, while letting go of judgment as if your life depends on it.*
>
> – Dr. Jon Kabat-Zinn

Adult coloring books topped the Amazon.com best-seller lists in 2015 and will likely still be there for years to follow. Why are so many adults seeking out circles and patterns collected in a book to color? People want to de-stress. Period. And coloring creates mindfulness, which is a technique that manages thoughts and feelings with focus and relaxation.

"I've been busy!" We hear ourselves say it in conversation, not even sure ourselves what that means exactly. Whatever it means, we must be productive. Right?

With the pace of our world, our minds are constantly going, mostly without our awareness.

Stress can come from our environment, but mostly it comes from our mind.

There comes a time, or perhaps a breaking point, when leaders know it's time to be alone. To regroup. To remember who we are, and why we are doing what we're doing. Being alone, whether it be centering, praying, exercising, or meditating, becomes something that not only relaxes our mind and body but makes us better leaders.

In essence, it is getting to a point where we have reached a deeper connection than fast-paced emails, screen clicks, scrolls down, informational skims, and quick how-are-yous in passing.

It's like this – a mind full:

We create conscious thoughts and expectations and beliefs, which take a chunk of mind space, but then most of us are not aware that subconsciously our brains are still working on the problem we've consciously stopped thinking about, so then we react unconsciously because by now we've put ourselves on autopilot, and while we just want peace we reach for our cell phones (or other addictive vice) because they do seem to focus (or numb) our attention but actually only perpetuate the stress reaction and feed it. (Deep breath.) Some, while connected to the virtual device in hand, perhaps end up scrolling through Amazon looking for the next fad that will calm frayed nerves because we want a break. From ourselves. From our thoughts. And so people want to experience peace of mind and end up buying…coloring books.

What we really want is this – mindfulness:

Peace and calm.

Stress and relaxation responses

Your body has a stress response – it's called "fight or flight" – that was created to save your life as your system dumps adrenaline and sugar into your bloodstream and expands your blood vessels and speeds your heart rate. The brain releases cortisol into your system. This chemical, which is meant to save your life in threatening situations, is actually harming your body as it stays in this constant state of bodily stress over *perceived* threats, physical and emotional – basically fear.

Your body also has a relaxation response. Your heart rate slows and the amygdala in your brain, which prepares the body for escape or defense, is calmed. There isn't a need for self-preservation or survival. There are many techniques that trigger the relaxation response – meditation is the biggest scientifically proven technique. This can also be experienced with music, a warm bath, and yoga, to name a few.

The relaxation response has two elements:

1. Repetition

2. Disregard of other things that come to mind

Coloring repetitive patterns, among other practices, creates this relaxation response – which is actually our "normal" state of mind.

Be the moment

In rural Kansas, it is easy to take a trip in the car only to realize upon reaching the destination that most of the drive was totally missed. Driving can be a trigger for going inside the mind and allowing the body to go on autopilot. After all, managing the motor vehicle is habitual.

Sometimes looking forward to a short jaunt in order to "relax" can be the mind wanting to check out of the moment. By checking out of the present moment – even if that moment is in a car on a monotonous highway – a portion of life is missed. Spending time in the mind is really spending time in an illusion. While the world is passing by – literally outside the window in some cases – we are missing it because we're spending time somewhere else in our head.

Music can have this effect as well. It can evoke strong emotional responses that take us back in our mind to a time when those emotions were created. It can also stop incessant thinking and create presence with the beat, the words or, as a friend of mine says, it can "call our spirit to attention." This means that fully experiencing the moment can be spiritual as it surpasses the mind. It's beyond thinking.

Having a mind full depletes energy and engagement.

Being mindful increases energy and engagement.

When our mind is where our body is, we are aligned with our fullest energy and engagement in the present moment or task at hand. Energy is wasted when the mind is honed in on the past or constantly predicting the future.

In the 2006 movie "Peaceful Warrior," a gymnast prepares for an Olympic moment. The video plays muted images of the gymnast in preparation for this moment while a verbal exchange between him and his coach ensues. The coach asks the question, "Where are you?" to which the gymnast answers, "Here."

"What time is it?"

"Now."

"What are you?"

"This moment."

Connecting with the present moment and being "here" instead of somewhere in your mind is the beginning of connecting fully in awareness. Feeling regret or anxiety is an indication of past or future thinking – moments that do not exist. The past did exist, but while it was happening it was "now." The future will exist, but while you're experiencing it, it'll be "now." Keeping our minds where our bodies are is mindfulness in the making.

Meditation is a purposeful way to recondition the mind from incessant thinking to peace and full engagement. It sculpts the brain in a similar way people sculpt their muscles and train their bodies (like a gymnast) to reshape, reform, and perform exactly as they have been conditioned.

Leave that should alone

"Shoulding and guilt no longer have a place in my life."

My reply to a family member made my own ears perk up. When the words spilled out of my mouth I hadn't known they were coming, so to my surprise, the truth of them lit me up inside! It was true! What freedom!

If the past is brought into the present, true mindfulness isn't happening. Words that indicate the past is affecting the present are: *should have, wish, can't, need to, have to.* These words indicate expectations that were more than likely created in a past experience. There is an undertone of regret, which is indicative of the past.

If the future is the focus instead of the present, words to listen for are: *what if, hope, maybe, I don't know.* These words indicate uncertainty. Anxiety or fear are the undertones and lack of control is indicative of future thinking.

Of course we learn from the past and there is a time for recalling it, but dwelling there with feelings that make the present moment elusive is when awareness becomes important. Planning for the future is responsible, but if the plans for what that future looks like consume you more than the moment you are in, then awareness is essential. Your life is always this moment.

Choose a practice

Be intentional to be aware of what is causing your stress response. If possible, remove it. If it's not possible to remove it, then strengthen your relaxation response. Not only are the health benefits significant, so is the evolution of your Greatest Self.

Choose a practice for reconditioning relaxation. Adult coloring books are one option. Another proven practice is meditation. You need only go as far as Google to find hundreds of hits about the benefits and increase of this practice in the West. Study after study has proven this practice to be scientifically sound in the way of neuroplasticity.

Another trend on the rise is float tanks, also known as sensory deprivation tanks. The tanks hold about 12 inches of water warmed to body temperature with 1,000 pounds of Epsom salt. The salt allows the body to stay afloat with zero effort. It's an anti-gravity, letting-go, sensory deprivation experience. Sixty minutes of floating is supposed to have the same benefits as four hours of deep meditation. There is no light, no sound, and no external distraction. It's like floating in outer space and allows nothing but space to be experienced. Namely, the space between your ears.

For some, this can sound scary, claustrophobic, and downright strange. Rightly so, this is a unique experience. In preparation before my first float I told myself to let go, let go some more…and then even more. Now, I float monthly for 60-90 minutes. (Followed by a massage! I've been known to say that heaven on earth exists on the corner of Douglas and Glendale.)

Be intentional to be mindful by not glorifying "being busy" and just experience "being". Your evolution depends on it.

Taken by: Nathan Peter-Grzeszczak Buhr

Sixty minutes in a float tank is said to have the same benefits as four hours of deep meditation.

"What are you counting?" my husband asks.

I wasn't counting. I was actually spelling on my fingertips to make a word fit by the number of letters or repeated letters, and I didn't realize I was doing it. He caught me again.

I reply, "A word from earlier," and we chuckle.

...

Walking from my dorm at college to the main building where my classes were held, I strode down the same sidewalk, careful to alternate steps so as not to step on cracks. If my stride was off and the crack was likely to end beneath my foot, I'd take a longer step to miss it. Of course if I did step on the crack, I'd be sure to step on the next one with the other foot to "even it out."

I've counted windows and found patterns in my mind while waiting, pumped gas intentionally to end the price with a 5 or 0, tapped my teeth together in a certain order – depending on the phrase or word my brain picked up and ran with, and spelled words on my fingertips in a specific way.

These behaviors began unconsciously and lasted into my late 20s. Over time I realized what my mind was doing. When I was not fully focused, my mind would catch onto something and repeat it over and over, and in a way, I'd have "peace of mind." That unconscious behavior distracted me. I spent a lot of time in my head without realizing it. There was something obsessive and compulsive about the way my mind worked, and I kept it to myself. Unless someone was on to these little quirks, I kept them hidden.

When I did finally talk about it with my family, I found out my dad and one of my sisters had similar behaviors. The two times (this makes three!) I've talked about this quirky brain behavior, people have labeled it as "weird" or something "crazy," and I learned to keep the quirks quiet. (On the up side, I developed a great appreciation for people who had quirks themselves. If you're one of them, I'm high-fiving you right now.)

After learning about stress and relaxation responses, I identified the counting and "evening out" as a way my brain would create its own relaxation response. It was repetitive thinking while disregarding other things coming to mind. In a way, my brain thought it was protecting me. Because I hadn't learned about mindfulness, it created a way to keep scary thoughts from coming to mind – and it never allowed a place for silence.

Over the past few years, I can count on one hand – ironically! – how many times I find myself lost in counting. Being fully aware and fully present moment to moment by practicing mindfulness, incorporating meditation, and floating have been influential in reconditioning my mind to be still.

And stillness is wonderful.

Life versus life experience

> *"...the deepest level of communication is not communication, but communion. It is wordless. It is beyond words, and it is beyond speech and beyond concept."*
>
> – Thomas Merton

My dad, whose body housed cancerous cells, sat on the couch in his home one afternoon with me right beside him. It was eight months after his diagnosis of pancreatic cancer and three months before I'd watch him take his last breath.

That afternoon Mom attempted a quick getaway by spending an afternoon with friends, and I happily drove up to be with Dad. As with most pancreatic patients, Dad's final year of life was riddled with pain. From intense, writhing pain to daily movement pain, he constantly had a divided mind. He tried to be present with us, but I knew he was doing everything he could to ignore the pain that kept screaming for attention.

That afternoon on the couch Dad told me, "I'm sorry I'm not very good company." The TV was on, but neither of us was watching it – it was just a short mindless distraction if we wanted one. To set the encounter straight I told him, "Dad, you don't have to entertain me. You don't even have to talk to me. I'm happy to just be here sitting with you."

He went on regretfully, "OK...Ohh..." he groaned, "...your mom shouldn't have to be going through this."

I understood what he was doing – he was sorry to be a burden. Sorry that his pain was bringing the rest of us pain. But I also saw it differently.

"Dad," I said, "Mom *is* going through this, and she's doing a good job." With complete sincerity and love I continued, "Wishing that something *wasn't* happening that *is* happening isn't helpful for you."

Dad reclined his side of the couch. He took off his glasses and set them on his belly. He folded his hands, rested them next to his glasses, laid his head back and with resolve said, "...You're right." Then he closed his eyes and drifted off to sleep.

For the next hour and a half I sat next to my dad and watched him sleep. It was one of the most profound times in my 36 years with him, and we never spoke a word. I sat fully aware of the aliveness of my dad and fully aware of my own.

There is something about being face to face with mortality. Sure, I knew I wasn't going to "lose" my dad (he would just pass through the very thin veil where everything returns to original form), and I refused to say he "lost a battle" to anything, but I did know that I wouldn't have him in this form forever. I wouldn't be able to touch him, look in his eyes, or listen to his hearty laugh during an on-going conversation. So my awareness of this gave me a moment of clarity I'll never forget: aliveness.

Trying to convey that moment attempting to use words feels limiting. Words cannot describe it. They can point you in the direction of "it," but unless you've sat fully aware in aliveness, the fullness of this moment slips by.

Communion is the deepest level of communication. Being *with* someone at this level is essentially *being* them. There's a connection, a Oneness, between life forms – and under that form (in whatever shell you find yourself), Life itself is there. You don't have to search for It. You cannot purchase It. You don't have to do anything to deserve It.

A life experience is something we have. Life is something we are, and glimpses of Life can be uncovered by practicing mindfulness – in the words of Dr. Kabat-Zinn, by *"paying attention to the present moment with intention, while letting go of judgment as if your life depends on it."*

Practice seeing things just as they are – not as you are. Practicing being fully present in every moment, in communion with Life, and let your mind rest.

This is the ultimate relaxation response – resting in God.

My dad a few months before diagnosed with cancer.

Dad about 10 months after diagnosis. I always wondered what he was thinking here.

Study Chapter Seven

Overview/Key Ideas:

- Mindfulness is not having a mind full of stuff.
- Meditation, a practice to increase mindfulness, is purposeful and intentional.
- Being mindful increases energy and engagement.
- Connecting with the present moment and being "here" instead of somewhere in the mind is the beginning of connecting fully in awareness.

Discussion Questions:

- As you read Chapter 7, what stood out to you and why?

- What keeps your mind full the most?

- How might electronics contribute to a mind full?

- What does mindfulness mean to you? How do you practice it?

- What are some benefits of mindfulness?

- How does "shoulding" or guilt impact your satisfaction or hold you back?

- What is one mindful practice you would like to implement in your life?

- When do you feel most at peace?

- What would be impacted if your organization cultivated mindfulness?

INspired Action

- For the next two minutes, practice mindfulness. Start by taking three deep breaths through your nose and out your mouth. Quiet your mind. Feel the contact points where your body meets your chair. Listen for any sounds in the room and focus on them. Look around and view something like it's the first time you've noticed it. Study it without any thought about it. Bring this practice into seemingly mundane tasks throughout your day (washing the dishes, driving, folding laundry, standing in line, eating breakfast, and so on.)
- Check your phone or email only two times a day. Intentionally leave your electronics in another room at home or at a distance at work. Note how your day flows without habitual use.

Chapter 8

Who is on Your Team?

You become the average of the five people you spend the most time with.

– Jim Rohn

Look around. Who are the five people you spend the most time with?

When I went to college, I hit the ground running. Well, actually it was passing, hitting and blocking. I was part of a volleyball team. A group. A collective unit. When I stood on the court, I could look around and see five teammates at any given time.

Anyone who has played sports knows how vibes within a team affect the outcome. And perhaps the vibes among a team can far outweigh the numbers on a scoreboard, leaving winning and losing an illusionary frame of reference.

I can't tell you the scores of specific games or an overall career wins and losses record, but I can tell you how much I enjoyed each particular year by the vibe I remember feeling. The experience of being in that group infused me with purpose, connection, and motivation.

Playing sports offers a multitude of life lessons. For one, relationships become the crux of the game, and in the game *of life*, you can choose who you want on your team.

Why not build an anabolic team? One that inspires, motivates, supports, and shares in your vision of who you believe you are and how you believe the world works? Better yet, why not also include those who will lovingly challenge those beliefs if it is obvious they're not serving you?

Here are considerations while discerning key players for your team:

Be aware of your own vibes.

Energy attracts like energy. If you keep finding yourself feeling drained or surrounded by complaining or feeling held back, be aware of how you're contributing to it.

Likewise, if you find yourself energized and enthusiastic, be aware of the dynamics around you. Creating vibes of greatness begins with being in tune with those vibes in the first place.

Make a shift in your own internal perception of yourself and others, and you'll attract people with the same contagious energy who want to join your team.

Listen to your own words.

Successful people are impeccable with their words. How we speak *to* each other and *about* each other determines the quality of our relationships, and relationships are significant to success.

I learned this principle when I began a new teaching job. One colleague befriended me quickly the summer before the school year began, and I found her to be very warm and inviting. On an in-service day when faculty was gathering for beginning-of-the-year informational meetings, another colleague approached me with a disparaging "warning" from an administrator that I might want to "stay away" from the colleague who had previously shown me much welcome and support. From that day on I felt distrust toward the administrator and the message deliverer, a teacher in my hall, from whom my first impression was negativity toward another faculty member. It just rubbed me wrong. It was a typecast from Day 1, and I never quite got my bearings for the integrity of leadership in that district. I felt that if I was friendly and had a good relationship with the colleague, I'd be seen in the same light administration saw her, but if I didn't follow my heart and be kind and loving, I'd be going against my own integrity of how I want to treat others.

What I learned over the next few years working in that environment was that gossip is a dividing force. And I know that what Jack Canfield says below is true:

> *When you speak ill of another to anyone else, it may temporarily bond*

you to that other person, but it creates a lasting impression in the other that you are a person who gossips negatively about others. That other person will always be wondering – even if unconsciously – when you will turn that verbal poison against them. It will erode the sense of deep trust in you.[1]

The biggest cost of gossiping, according to Canfield, is that it robs you of a clear mind. He says gossiping is like releasing a computer virus into your mind, causing it to think a little less clearly every time.

Words have the power to build up, edify, strengthen, and empower, or they can tear down, separate, reject, and be empty. If you want to be a leader who builds deep and lasting relationships and empowers others, gossip must be vanquished.

What evaluation criteria do you use for tryouts?

How are you basing the cuts for your team? Are external factors important like: *Our location is convenient for friendship. They're attractive. They make a lot of money and have a lot of accolades.* Or is something more internally motivating like: *They love, empower, and appreciate others. They are inspiring and challenging.*

The measurement you use will come back to you. The ego loves to side with those who seem more admired by others in order to get in on the attention itself. Likewise, it may retract from someone who may not seem as popular. If you want to be seen for who you are, then evaluate others for who they are – at their core. When you're open, you may discover a team member you didn't consider before.

To have energetic, honest, and caring vibes, look past the external and pay attention to the way a person processes life. It's the difference between someone who participates and enjoys the game, and one who sits in the stands complaining about the way others are playing.

How much time are you allowing key players in the game?

Be intentional about your contacts and connections. Carve out a few hours a week or a month to reconnect, repurpose, and re-motivate. Make time for those who strengthen you.

It is also highly likely you are a key player for your own key players. Make time for those you strengthen. This is not to be confused with those who drain you! There is a difference between giving to someone and feeling drained afterward and giving to someone and walking away with even more energy.

One very thoughtful woman I coach is conscientious about not wanting me to feel this way. I've explained to her that after our calls I feel more energized than before I picked up the phone. Talking with people who are working to improve themselves in an open and authentic way is not even a comparison to someone who simply complains.

A Vacation from unhappiness

After a few rough days with our 4-year-old son, the opportunity to present this concept showed up. I purchased a travel bag with goodies to give to each of the kids for a long drive to a neighboring state. Knowing they were "vacation" bags, the kids knew they would have to wait. On the third day of "a few rough days," my son's bag became the topic of whining. (At this point, anything would've done it.) I pulled him onto my lap and snuggled him and said, "Buddy, it seems like you want to be unhappy. Do you?" The boy whose first word is always "No!" didn't say anything. That moment was the end of the three-day struggle. If a 4-year-old can realize the suffering he is creating for himself, then anyone can step back and re-evaluate.

Nobody really *desires* unhappiness. It's just a frame of mind that feels most comfortable, so slipping into it feels natural. Do you know people who just seem to want to be unhappy? Are you one of them?

When you're conscious about the team surrounding you as well as your own contribution, the game of life flows with so much more ease and enjoyment.

"I'm not a human being having a spiritual experience, I'm a spiritual being having a human experience," he said, clinching my intuitive feeling that including a story about a successful high school football coach would fit into the content of this chapter well. In fact, it was at this point I felt the familiar energetic rush and goosebumps that raise themselves to attention when I feel a bigger purpose in progress.

"We're just renting these bodies," he went on.

Are you serious? I explained to Brandon more about the metaphor carried throughout the book – likening those who will read this book to an acorn, an exterior body functioning as is but with an interior far beyond the limitations of its temporary shell.

He already got it, and I was pumped.

When he explained something his administrator said, "The magic isn't the football team on Friday nights. It's the fans, the crowd, and *everything else* around it," I instantly connected. While I did learn about the culture of a football team in a school that falls into the largest classification in the state of Kansas, it was the excitement about *everything else* that compelled me most.

The success of a football team will be noted on some pages in this book, but the magic to tune into is what happens when people communicate their greatness…like when Brandon shared with me that quote about having a human experience as a spiritual being made him stop and think about "who I was and why I was here."

That's the magic. There's something bigger than football. There's something bigger than a human experience.

"I don't really read books about football," he said "I mostly read inspirational books." (After we swapped authors and titles, I assured him he'd also enjoy one called "An INspired Evolution.")

The stats and numbers and wins and losses are typically what constitute "success," but what INspired Leadership is about and what Brandon conveyed is that there is also success beyond wins and losses. Inspiration isn't as easy to quantify as wins and losses, but it can be uncovered and discovered within them.

The year before Brandon stepped into the head coach position, the football record was 0-9. Part of which, he suggested, was a change in four different head coaches in four years. There was too much downtime and a lack of stability. His first year improved to 1-8 and then the next seven of eight years the team made state semifinals and won state twice. The statistics are outward reflections of inward attention. This inspiring connection clicked when he described the meaning behind a Chinese Bamboo Story told to kindergarteners in his district and repeated throughout middle school and continued in high school.

"Love the stuff that's hidden," he told me "Underground is a giant root system."

The Bamboo Story tells of a farmer whose job is to water a seed in the ground. He continues to water and care for the seed for a year, but there is still no evidence of a plant. He continues in persistence to water and care for the "plant," although he cannot see fruit of his labor. This happens for four years! Day after day, night after night, there is nothing tangible to show above ground for the consistent work of the farmer. However, during the fifth year the tree sprouts. It grows up to 80 feet in five weeks! For a tree to grow that height in such a short period of time requires a system of roots underground that had to be prepared and able to support such rapid growth.

So *love the stuff that's hidden*, Brandon shared, and by the time those kindergarteners are juniors and seniors playing varsity football, they are stable and ready for the opportunity to burst onto the scene, to expand as deep and wide as their roots will allow. This translates to the football field, of course, but also throughout their daily lives.

Another embedded principle in the football program is to "win the day."

"That doesn't mean just Friday nights or in the weight room," he said, "it means to win the day at home, in the classroom, in everything you're doing. Never take a moment off. We teach this at a young age and build off it.

"The first thing our program needed was discipline and then stability…stability to stand behind. We created a culture to not disappoint anybody in our family. That means making right choices, work ethic, punctuality, and what all that entails. Trust is big in discipline. I'd throw out that trust word about every minute I was coaching in the beginning."

I asked about the relationships among his coaching staff.

"We're all friends. We all get along and hang out. The first thing I tell them is what I tell our players: Family comes first. We talk about faith and family, and then school, and then football when it's football season. If you want your team to be a family and create a culture, you have to represent that," he said. "My main thing on leadership and our coaches is what we call servant leadership. We're not here to create a dictatorship or anything. We're here to serve others: our community, our school, the players, and each other."

He continued, "We've been lucky enough to have a program that has coaches with passion and energy who aren't here to be in charge but to teach life lessons."

I wanted to know more about Brandon personally and who he was and how he turned around a program. What he said about himself was that 1. He would not let anyone out-work him and 2. He aims to stay humble.

And true to staying humble, he talked more about his administrator than himself.

"We have an unbelievable school with an unbelievable leader," he said. "He created a family within a school of 1,900 students. He started the "Green is Magic" principle that the football program adopted, and the whole school has adopted it.

One story he told to emphasize the culture of family began when the administrator called an impromptu "family meeting" and brought everybody, roughly 1,900 people, into the big gym. The kids knew they were in trouble because of broken stands during an away football game. The student section had jumped on the stands during the game, leaving them damaged.

"When the administrator got in there and took the mic, the whole school – teachers, students, everybody! – was quiet, so quiet you could hear a pin drop. For 15 minutes he talked about disappointment, and he took away an anticipated event for the student body and told them they had to earn it back. Afterward, he handed the mic to the assistant principal…and everyone clapped.

"Kids were volunteering. Not just the football team, the whole student body. Everybody supports everybody.

"There used to be 4-5 fights a week in our school, but this year there were maybe 4-5 fights total. Our administrator's position was very pivotal in the culture of the school. We can get buy-in from a football team… and to get buy-in in a school of 1,900 is amazing."

Besides "Green is Magic" and "Win the Day," the football program wants its family to "Bring the Juice."

"We want them to have fun and enjoy it. Bringing the juice is all about bringing the energy – bringing positive energy and having a positive flow. Now we don't have to discipline. We just focus on enjoying what we're doing. It makes hard work fun, and it's easier to see your vision," he explained.

The team captains read "The Carpenter" by Jon Gordon about servant leadership – serving others and serving their purpose. The whole team is reading "The Energy Bus" by Gordon as well, and weekly motivational meetings are conducted to break down the book by chapters, tell stories, and include faith.

I asked Brandon what the best part about all of this is for him. He said that once you have the foundation, it's ingrained in your school, and you can start taking steps forward.

"We're all about positive energy," he said.

...

For the record, INspired Leadership is, too… from the INside out.

Bamboo trees take five years to develop a deep and sturdy root system before shooting 80 feet straight up in five short weeks.

Study Chapter Eight

Overview/Key Ideas:

- Create a team that INspires, motivates, supports, and shares a vision.
- Your words create energy.
- Be intentional about making time for those who strengthen you.

Discussion Questions:

- As you read Chapter 8, what stood out to you and why?

- Think about the people you spend the most time with. What are common characteristics?

- Gossip is a dividing force. Where do you see gossip ruining relationships and damaging cultures? How can you help eliminate this?

- Energy attracts like energy. How intentional are you in your interactions? What type of energy are you spreading?

- Share about one relationship where you feel supported, INspired, or motivated. What specific actions occur in that relationship?

- How do you make time for those who INspire you? How are you INspiring others?

- How are relationships in your organization?

INspired Action

- Successful people are impeccable with their words. How we speak to one another and about each other determines the quality of our relationships, and relationships are significant to success. Choose a significant relationship and send a gesture of gratitude to that person by the end of the day (card, text, email, phone call, etc.).

Chapter 9

Something More

You must love in such a way that the person you love feels free.

– Thich Nhat Hanh

If you want to be an inspiration, start loving. Love your life, love your job, love your kids, love yourself, love your neighbor, love your failures…love exactly where you are in this moment. The illusion that something else will satisfy you is just that – an illusion. Goals and intentions are wonderful to create, but loving the process is what makes the most impact because love is what sets us free.

In a nutshell, INspired Leadership really encompasses one thing. In dealing with others, and ourselves, the biggest insight is that whatever we do overflows from who we are. In discovering and uncovering and unveiling the greatness inside you, what you're really finding is that your capacity for love exceeds your form, and what you can do in form is only as deep and wide as your being immersed and rooted in love. Love is what it's about.

In most of us there is an underlying insatiable quest for more, something beyond ourselves. We're looking for something beyond what is right here – wherever here is for you. In this quest, people climb a ladder for years to reach some pinnacle of success only to find it wasn't there. Some make purchases thinking the next item is "it," but it isn't. Some will scour the earth for a mate only to find out that Hollywood has romanticized relationships and that sharing life with another person comes with little annoyances and monotonous everyday duties.

Something more isn't outside, it's inside, perfectly hidden in plain sight.

It's been said that when asked how he carved his famous statue of David, Michelangelo replied, "I just chipped away everything that wasn't David."

Did Michelangelo create the statue, or was David already there? For a man who could see something more than the external piece of marble, David only needed to be uncovered.

Less is more

You don't have to try so hard to become something more. You only need to carve away what you are NOT to be left with what's already there. You'll be naked, like David, and not hidden by labels, judgments, noise, ego, rules or expectations. You will be authentic and vulnerable and very strong.

You can have more and you can be more, but you will discover and uncover it when "more" is no longer something for which you search outside of yourself.

The chase

This principle also surfaced as I learned about Brandon's story, which he describes here:

My whole athletic and coaching career, I thought I was chasing a state championship. We fell short many times in the state semifinals. My whole life I kind of felt like a failure because I was chasing that dream. I felt that in order to feel true success we had to win a state championship.

In 2013, we finally reached that stage and finally reached what I thought I was wanting my whole life: a state championship. I was the last one to leave the field. I walked off the field with my wife and kids and turned to my wife and stopped. The feeling that I was feeling was not what I'd expected. I felt something I didn't think I would feel.

Before that moment I thought the feeling of winning a state championship was the ultimate goal for a head coach and would bring great joy and fulfillment. But in that moment, I felt disappointed.

Don't get me wrong, I was very excited to see our players and fans so excited! It just hit me what coaching and successful coaching was all about.

Walking off the field, I knew then what my calling truly was and what it was not. It was not about winning state championships…I left that field feeling disappointed that I had spent the majority of my life feeling like I wasn't fulfilled by not winning what I just won. I realized then that it wasn't about getting to the top. It wasn't about reaching that goal that I thought was my ultimate goal. My calling was about the process and the relationships that I built reaching that goal.

After that, my mindset switched. I wasn't chasing a state championship anymore, I was living in the moment and enjoying the relationships and loving the process that it took to get there.

Because of my new mindset, 2015 was way different for me when we won the state championship again.

Walking off the field a second time, I recognized the same feeling of unfulfillment, but the second go-around I knew it was going to be there. That same feeling was there, but the emptiness wasn't. I knew that a state championship didn't define me as a successful coach. It just took winning the first one to realize that.

You are already something more

More than likely, you're chasing something. In reality, the chase – the process – *is* the something. If we hold out for an event, a person, an accomplishment, or a result to define us as "great," then we've missed the point, which is to love every bit of every moment.

It is common to be concerned with results. How else do we have data to determine growth and success? In business and in education, evidence feels essential, and the bottom line, final sales, and test scores become the basis of success. These are important results but not what is most important to the development of a person.

Love your purpose

Your greatest fulfillment does not come from promoting yourself despite many venues appearing to be saying it does. Deepest fulfillment comes in loving and empowering others.

There is a time and place to replenish and be led and restored beside still waters, and then there is a time to lead others to their own still waters. The greatest selves are using whatever platform in which they find themselves to inspire the greatness in others. It is love that drives the fullest people. Not the dollar. Not fame. Not the house. Not the boat. Not the stuff. Although those can be motivating factors, they will not bring to a person what aligning to purpose will bring. They won't even compare.

Love your work

To some, a job is something that must be done to pay the bills. An analytical view of this might sound like, "This is my job. I go do my work, and I get paid for it. I use the money to get this and that…" Or some might view their job as an identity, "I am a (insert role title here)." It is the title that determines significance. There is an importance associated with a role and the position itself is what gives meaning, not necessarily the work.

Then there are those in tune with their purpose and what they do flows from an alignment. These are people who have "a calling" and find meaning within all daily encounters. Like Brandon's football team, they not only win the day, they win the moments.

Work can define you, or you can define your work. INspired Leadership is about *you*. Your work will overflow from who you are.

The picture below illustrates alignment with purpose.

www.shechangeseverythingshetouches.com

Often I'll ask people, "What makes you come alive? What invigorates you?" From there, enthusiasm and passion will automatically course through your work because it is aligned to who you are at your core. You'll gain energy as you work!

Love your failures

Thomas Edison is said to have failed 1,000 times before the light bulb was finally created. Apparently when asked about his failures, he said, "The light bulb was an invention with 1,000 steps."

How you view your "failures" will determine how you continue to create. If setbacks are viewed as unacceptable, if fear of making mistakes becomes limiting, or if they're seen as a confirmation for belief in your own inability, your greatest self will not fully emerge. By overcoming the fear of making the mistake in the first place, you allow a place for love to pick you back up, dust you off, and send you along your way again.

Failure and success go hand in hand. In fact, some of the most "successful" people would argue they coexist. Most people quit when experiencing failure instead of riding it out as part of the process. Loving failure as much as loving success will always produce an evaluation that leads to growth.

When fear gets in the way

Recognizing fear is recognizing an opportunity to further evolve.

Everyone has encountered fear. The size of one's comfort zone plays a role in the amount of materialized fear, and the amount of time spent traveling outside that zone plays another. Comfort zones are comfortable, so not wanting to leave is reasonable. The time to entertain fear as unreasonable is when you know it's stunting your growth.

INspired Leadership is about personal development. What we fear doing most is usually what we most need to do. Instead of wishing something could be easier, wish you were better, more developed, and certainly flowing with the greatness inside you.

No matter the reason fear shows up, the fact is it does. Unknown outcomes trigger fear – it is uncertainty of the future that limits, confuses, or stops us.

There's a scene in the 2013 movie "After Earth" when Will Smith's character has a revelation about fear that he shares with his son:

"Fear is not real. The only place fear exists is in our thoughts…It is a product of our imagination causing us to fear things that do not exist in the present and may not ever exist. That is near insanity… Don't misunderstand me, danger is very real. But fear is a choice."

More than likely, fear will be your biggest obstacle in discovering your greatness. For an INspired Evolution, ultimately a choice in your evolution must include what you want to do with it.

Death, failure & what other people think

In sources I've read, the top fear people report is speaking in front of groups. Followed by that is death. More people (at least those polled) would rather die than speak in public. One of these fears is literal death, and the other induces feelings of dread that can make people wish they were dead.

The feelings that create a desire for something other than what is happening is where the ego comes in. Egos are afraid of diminishing.

What if I screw this up? What if they laugh at me? What if people disagree with my message, or worse, what if they hate me?

If we're afraid of rejection, then fear is an illusion created in the mind by thoughts about the real "danger." You won't die. Your ego will just get smaller. This experience actually makes room for your greatness to be fully known!

A way to eliminate the illusion of fear

The ego loves illusion. The reality is that beyond form, nobody is superior to another. (For some of you, that last sentence will be bothersome.) When relating to others from this position, true authentic connection occurs. Dying to ego (or dying to self, as Jesus put it[1]) is the birthing of fearlessness because what is real cannot be threatened.

One of my favorite practices to expose the ego's illusion is by Eckhart Tolle in "A New Earth":

> *A powerful spiritual practice is consciously to allow the diminishment of ego when it happens without attempting to restore it. I recommend that you experiment with this from time to time. For example, when someone criticizes you, blames you, or calls you names, instead of immediately retaliating or defending yourself – do nothing. Allow the self-image to remain diminished and become alert to what that*

feels like deep inside you. For a few seconds, it may feel uncomfortable, as if you had shrunk in size. Then you may sense an inner spaciousness that feels intensely alive. You haven't been diminished at all. In fact, you have expanded. You may then come to an amazing realization: When you are seemingly diminished in some way and remain in absolute non-reaction, not just externally but also internally, you realize that nothing real has been diminished, that through becoming "less," you become more. Through becoming less (in the ego's perception), you in fact undergo an expansion and make room for Being to come forward. True power, who you are beyond form, can then shine through the apparently weakened form.[2]

True power, who you are beyond form, can finally shine through when ego has been exposed and then chipped away to uncover the authentic, true, and significant self withIN.

It is *this* place from where all inspiring things flow.

1

"At some points in life everything comes together like you were made just for that moment."

My friend Trish told me that. I just didn't expect it to happen during a funeral. And definitely not my dad's funeral. And definitely not while I was standing up speaking in front of hundreds of mourners while still mourning myself.

I told the group that was gathered that I put on my boots that morning because if I was going to be shaking, I was going to be shaking in my boots.

Flash back 25 years prior to that moment and I was sitting in the same church with my family, fourth pew from the back, and I had a vision of myself speaking at the pulpit. It was a clear image in my mind that simultaneously reached my heart. I let the vision fall back into the recesses of my mind. *Why (and when) would I ever be speaking from that location?*

The vision began to resurface when cancer joined our family and eight months into the journey Dad began to plan his own service. He never asked me to speak and although the thought crossed my mind, I didn't give it much merit. I recalled the vision I'd had as a little girl, but there wasn't a casket in the vision. Since that was the case, the idea of healing was settled in my heart, and *that* is what I'd be talking about in front of my parents' church. I'd gladly be talking about it in front of everyone!

The vision began to become clearer when, about a month before Dad took his final breath, Mom informed us that he had chosen to be cremated.

Cremated. No casket.

So there was never a casket? My internal dialogue became a conversation between what I believed was happening while uncovering what was really happening.

What other reason would I be standing in front of that church if not to celebrate healing? *Even though there was no casket, Dad was not standing beside me in the vision either...*

Over the course of a year, what else would I speak about but what had been downloaded into me when I was most open to receiving it? *I opened my eyes to new perceptions because Dad was about to close his...*

So I prepared a talk. The message was already inside me. And clad in boots, I shook as I waited in the front pew to deliver it. My hands sweat, my heart beat fast, and my stomach was tense as I stood up and approached the pulpit in my vision.

This moment never included a casket.

And just like the metaphor I have continued to drag across these pages, greatness emerged. Not because others recognized it but because *I* recognized it.

When I looked out at the faces in the crowd, I loved that moment. I loved my dad. I loved my family. I loved Life. Death reminded me that Life matters, and I was given an opportunity to awaken anyone who had come to the service asleep.

Everything in life seemed to come together in that moment like I was made for it, and this is what I knew that day: Our beginnings and our ends are known. And if that is so, then every moment in between matters. Every thing. Every person. Every encounter. All of it matters. We only need to be present enough to fully experience every Moment because *this* is where greatness exists.

This moment is where an INspired Evolution begins.

Study Chapter Nine

Overview/Key Ideas:

- Greatness is already within you. It only needs to be discovered, uncovered, and unveiled.
- Satisfaction in life is not exclusive to reaching external goals.
- Instead of trying hard to become something more, intentionally carve away what you are not.
- Authenticity and vulnerability strengthen self-confidence and relationships.
- Deepest fulfillment comes in loving and empowering others.
- Honoring failures allows for more creativity.
- Fear can be the biggest obstacle in discovering greatness.
- In dealing with others, and ourselves, the biggest INsight is that whatever we do overflows from who we believe we are.

Discussion Questions:

- As you read Chapter 9, what stood out to you and why?

- What invigorates you and makes you come alive?

- How does fear keep you from experiencing your greatness?

- What is your "calling"?

- Discuss a time when you were aware you were chasing "more" and you still didn't find satisfaction when you achieved it. How did this experience impact you?

- How comfortable are you with vulnerability and authenticity?

INspired Action

- Oftentimes we focus on what we do not have instead of what we do have. You can have more and you can be more, but you will discover and uncover it when "more" is no longer something for which you search outside of yourself.
    - Identify times when you say "I'm not enough" or "this isn't enough" (e.g., if only I had more time, had a different boss, lived in a bigger house, had more money, had a different job, etc.). Stop and tell yourself a different story. Reflect on this moment as enough and take action that is purposeful and meaningful.

Epilogue

There *is* something more, but it is nothing you can reach out and get. It is something you already have…and it's ready to grow.

Wherever you find yourself in this process, love the evolution. It is love that magnifies your greatness and loves that inspires and empowers others to discover and magnify their own greatness.

"There is a secret place. A radiant sanctuary. As real as your own kitchen. More real than that. Constructed of the purest elements. Overflowing with ten thousand beautiful things. Worlds within worlds. Forest, rivers. Velvet coverlets thrown over featherbeds, fountains bubbling beneath a canopy of stars. Bountiful forests, universal libraries. A wine cellar offering an intoxication so sweet you will never be sober again. A clarity so complete you will never again forget. This magnificent refuge is inside you. Enter. Shatter the darkness that shrouds the doorway…Believe the incredible truth that the Beloved has chosen you for His dwelling place – the core of your own being – because that is the single most beautiful place in all of creation."

– Maribai Starr

Notes

CHAPTER ONE

[1]Wayne Dyer. (n.d.). BrainyQuote.com. Retrieved April 4, 2016, from BrainyQuote.com Web site: http://www.brainyquote.com/quotes/quotes/w/waynedyer385865.html

[2]http://www.dictionary.com/browse/perfect

CHAPTER THREE

[1]1 John 4:20 (New International Version)

CHAPTER FOUR

[1]Rohr, Richard, *Falling Upward*. (San Francisco: Jossey-Bass, 2011).

[2]Some of Greg's language was edited out throughout this excerpt. If some words were to be the cause of passing over this book (or his story), we decided to give readers a choice. When I asked if he could describe some things in a different way, this was his response and the reason I left it true to him in the unabridged version of this book: *That's actually really tough because I can't think of any other way to describe it as well as that. It's torture. It makes you willing to do anything just to make it stop but it never does. Until you either go too far or you finally escape and in the end you never actually escape. I still have dreams about it; I still get reminded of the agony every time I hear a certain name or random event tied to any of it. It's a scar that's very difficult to hide.*

CHAPTER EIGHT

[1]Canfield, Jack, *The Success Principles.* (New York: HarperCollinsPublishers, Inc., 2005), 344.

CHAPTER NINE

[1]Matthew 16:24 (New International Version)

[2]Tolle, Eckhart, *A New Earth.* (New York: Plume, 2005), 215.

About INspired Leadership

The INL Team (from left to right): Rachel Thalmann, Tammy Fellers, Tamara Konrade, Meg Wilson, Mike Sanders

LIVE A LIFE YOU LOVE

Our mission is to assist you in magnifying your INner greatness. By increasing your awareness and uncovering thoughts and actions impeding your journey, you can create a life and culture you want.

INspired Leadership has trained thousands of individuals and a multitude of schools and organizations on energy, engagement, and leadership. Our work creates awareness causing internal shifts for individuals and organizations, which create external shifts without the chase.

All members are certified professional coaches, and all members have a passion for INspiring others to live a life as fulfilling as possible. We would love to know you!